Starz, the Musical

Book, Music & Lyrics by

Amy Shojai & Frank Steele

Performance rights for all materials contained herein
must be obtained from Shojai & Steele Plays
http://amyshojai.com/plays
Copyright © 2016-2017 by Amy Shojai, Frank Steele
ALL RIGHTS RESERVED/Music ASCAP Registered

STARZ, THE MUSICAL!

A Drama-dy
In Two Acts

903-868-1022 or 903-893-2039
ALL MUSIC REGISTERED VIA ASCAP

FURRY MUSE
PUBLISHING
PO BOX 1904, SHERMAN TX 75090

DIRECTOR'S NOTES

STARZ, THE MUSICAL is written especially with theater lovers in mind and explores theater from the ARTISTS' point of view. The actors give voice to a variety of performer characters in this hilarious and often moving "drama-dy" that seeks to edu-tain audiences about how and why artists come to the theater—and often stay for a lifetime. The complete show runs approximately two hours with an intermission. It can be performed with or without a break.

STARZ is a review format show, with a mix of funny to poignant scenes (with and without music). It was inspired by students and instructors attending the Texas Thespian Festival, and hearing the concerns, frustrations and joys theatrical artists share. The playwrights hope it will be widely used in productions open to a wide range of artists, from students to professionals, and especially in arts-funding endeavors.

CASTING NOTES

STARZ can be cast with any age performer, but age 12 to adult is recommended. This is an ensemble show, with no specific "stars" and addresses the issue of "type casting" in a realistic but also humorous way. Therefore, a mix of body types, ages and genders offers the most fun and flexibility.

The show can be mounted with as few as **12 ADULT SINGER/ACTORS** doubling roles, or **20 FEATURED PLAYERS** plus a **CHORUS**. All featured performers may also perform in group/ensemble numbers with solo phrases/choruses assigned individually as wished.

Suggested casting/doubling recommendations follow, but songs and scenes may be mixed and matched to best fit talents. Only a few are specifically male/female, with most open to either pending your best casting options.

CHARACTER BREAKDOWNS

DIRECTOR #1 (male/BARI or female/ALTO): Harshly critical and inflexible, also performs various VO. Sings the feature song MY WAY OR THE HIGHWAY, and DUELING DIRECTORS scene/song. May double **STAGE MANAGER.**

LANCE (male) or BLANCHE (female), a know-it-all who is "all that" and makes sure everyone knows. Features include nonsensical Q & A's and theater games.

DIRECTOR #2 (male/BARI or female/ALTO): Supportive and generous, has hidden insecurities. Performs various VO as needed. Features include BROKEN DREAMS monologue, DREAMS NEVER DIE song, and YOU'RE ENOUGH monologue. May double **CHANCE.**

CHOREOGRAPHER (male/BARI or female/ALTO): Generally supportive but focused on casting talents with dance skills. Featured in MY WAY OR THE HIGHWAY and scene/song DUELING DIRECTORS.

PIANIST (male or female): A talented rehearsal accompanist, MUST ACTUALLY PLAY PIANO. Funny, snarky character who has a love/hate relationship with other performers. Features include PIANO MAN monologue. May double as **VOCAL COACH** in DUELING DIRECTORS scene/song.

VOCAL COACH (male/TENOR or female/SOP): Generally supportive but focused on casting talents with vocal skills. Featured in MY WAY OR THE HIGHWAY and scene/song DUELING DIRECTORS.

BUBBA HUMPHREY (male/TENOR): Bubba's girlfriend dragged him to the theater. Despite initial reluctance, he starts to embrace the arts, especially after partnered with his leading lady (NOT his girlfriend). Features include WE'RE NOT BABIES, TALK DIRTY TO ME, I'M PERFECT and STAGE CRUSH scenes, and the song/waltz feature WHEN KISSES DON'T MATTER.

STAGE MANAGER (male or female): Strong, confident, no nonsense character, with lots of pride in ability. Features include RESPECT monologue, WE'RE NOT BABIES scene, and rap feature in WHEN TECHIES LET YOU DOWN song. May double as **DIRECTOR #1.**

SYDNEY POINDEXTER (female/SOP): Shy, soft spoken, and insecure, Poindexter has hidden depths and talents. Features include DUELING DIRECTORS song/scene, WE'RE NOT BABIES and STAGE CRUSH scenes, and song/dance feature WHEN KISSES DON'T MATTER.

BERTHA GETTS (female/MEZZO): An ingénue "type," with giggly, cheerleader perky personality. She struggles with auditions and is considered a bad cold reader, but she has hidden depths and yearns for meatier roles. Her features include the scene WE'RE NOT BABIES, the song STARZ, the scene/song DUELING DIRECTORS, and scene CRY, BABY, CRY.

TRIO (female): Typical girl backup singers, able to sing close three-part harmony. Featured in song I'M IN IT FOR THE BABES, backup trio in TECHIE RAP and various unassigned roles (the "girlfriend" or "casting director" or VO parts). All female players may supplement TRIO feature.

CHANDLER VON BARRYMORE (male/TENOR): Chance is a bit of a nerd, but gains confidence when he discovers the stage. He borders on being a stage hog and gets called on it by other actors in the scene WE'RE NOT BABIES. He's featured in the song I'M IN IT FOR THE BABES, and the scene I'M PERFECT. When doubling **DIRECTOR #2** offers nice character arc from "actor" to "director."

SOL (or ESMERELDA) "SHECKY" LIEBOWICZ (male/BARI or female/ALTO): Shecky is a class clown, constantly spouting bad jokes to hide his own insecurities. Features include BOOGIE WOOGIE LAFFS (two keys available) and the scene/song DUELING DIRECTORS and I'M PERFECT.

SHIRLEY ANN TEMPLER (female/MEZZO): Initially a reluctant performer, Shirley resents but also wants to please her stage mother. She fears she won't measure up to her mother's expectations. Features include the duet SPARKLE (with possible dance), STARZ song, and the scene/song DUELING DIRECTORS. She finds her happy place once joining the backstage crew in TECHIE RAP.

MOM (female/SOP): A frustrated performer, Mom lives her own dreams through her daughter Shirley. She's pushy and brash stage mother, and a bit jealous of her daughter's talent and opportunities. Features include the duet SPARKLE (with possible dance feature), STARZ song, the scene I'M PERFECT and the scene/song DUELING DIRECTORS.

DAD (male/TENOR): Percy Carlson is a fan of sports, fishing, and other "manly" pastimes, and completely puzzled by his son's interest in theater. He loves his son, and struggles to find common ground. Features include FATHER/SON scenes, and the song MAKE ME PROUD.

PERCIVAL WALLACE CARLSON III (male/TENOR): Wally loves the theater, and is determined to make it his life. He is talented but has stage fright and easily cracks under pressure. His family and especially his father don't understand. Features include the FATHER/SON scenes, the song STARZ, and song/dance feature WALTZING IN 4/4 TIME where Wally finally finds confidence.

VARIOUS ENSEMBLE performers to play techies & additional dancers/singers as needed.

VOCAL AND MOVEMENT REQUIREMENTS

Music consists of a variety of song styles from pop to boogy-woogie to big band and show tunes. The multiple verses offer lots of feature solo line opportunities. Solo numbers may have backup singers, and company numbers require two- to four-part harmonies. Most songs are easy mid-range tenor and alto lines.

Harmony mostly is written as "rounds" or combinations of melody lines. This keeps learning music simple for non-music-readers. A piano score for rehearsal is available, with show performance using a CD with full orchestration; a rehearsal piano/vocal CD can be provided. Vocal ranges from baritone (from low B) to soprano (to high G).

Strong dance ability is not required. Feature dance solos are encouraged when talents have that ability particularly in SPARKLE, WALTZING IN 4/4 TIME, and WHEN KISSES DON'T MATTER. Movement and choreography for ensemble numbers may be as simple or complex as needed that fits the talents. Fun, campy choreography particularly of **TRIO** for IN IT FOR THE BABES, and the group rap in WHEN TECHIES LET YOU DOWN and FIT THE SUIT is encouraged and enhances the characters and performance.

COSTUMES, PROPS/SET PIECES/STAGING

Costumes and props should suggest the character (STAGE MANAGER vs DIRECTOR vs CHOREOGRAPHER vs ACTOR). No special costuming or props are required, only what would be used during a normal audition/rehearsal process.

The show can be performed on a bare stage with actors entering/exiting from and interacting with the audience. Conversely, it can be staged on an existing set to infer the production in progress.

SCENES & SONGS

ACT 1

Scene 1: *Misfit*..Company
Scene 2: Slate..Company
Scene 3: *My Way, Or The Highway* ....3 Directors, Company
Scene 4: Father/Son #1..Dad, Wally
Scene 5: Theater Games #1...Lance
Scene 6: *Sparkle* ....Mom, Shirley
Scene 7: Know It All #1..Lance
Scene 8: Piano Man ....Pianist, Dir, Choreo, Mom, V-Coach, Singer
Scene 9: *Boogie Woogie Laffs* ....Shecky
Scene 10: Know It All #2...Lance
Scene 11: *In It For The Babes* ....Chance, Trio
Scene 12: Know It All #3 ....Lance
Scene 13: Babies...............Poind, Bertha, Stg Mng, Chance, Bubba, Wally
Scene 14: *Starz*..............................Bertha, Wally, Mom, Shirley
Scene 15: *Make Me Proud*......................Dad, Wally, Mom, Shirley
Scene 16: Talk Dirty To Me...............................Casting Dir, Bubba
Scene 17: Broken Dreams...Director #2
Scene 18: *Fit The Suit*..Company

ACT 2

Scene 1: *Dreams Never Die*...Director #2
Scene 2: I'm Perfect.........................Mom, Shirley, Shecky, Bubba
Scene 3: You're Enough..Director #2
Scene 4: *Waltzing In 4/4 Time*..Wally
Scene 5: Theater Games #2..Lance
Scene 6: Dueling Directors............VOs, Bertha, Shirley, Poind, Shecky
Scene 7: *Dueling Directors* ....Directors & Company
Scene 8: Know It All #4..Lance
Scene 9: Stage Crush..Poindexter, Bubba, VO
Scene 10: *When Kisses Don't Matter*.....................Poindexter, Bubba
Scene 11: Know It All #5..Lance
Scene 12: Cry Baby Cry........................Bertha, Shirley, Wally, VO
Scene 13: Respect...Stage Manager
Scene 14: *When Techies Let You Down* .... Company
Scene 15: Father/Son #2..Dad, Wally
Scene 16: *Starz Finale*..Company

PRODUCTION HISTORY

A table reading of the completed **STARZ, THE MUSICAL!** was first performed December 5, 2017 at HOPE ON HOUSTON, 901 E. Houston St., Sherman, Texas. Open auditions were held February 5-8, 2018, and the show cast with talented performers.

STARZ, THE MUSICAL full production was first staged and performed April 19, 20, 21, 2018 at The Rialto Theater, 426 West Main Street, Denison, TX (www.TheRialtoTheater.net). The originating cast and production staff are listed on the next page.

STARZ ORIGINAL CAST

WALLY……………………………………..	Alex Nield
GIRLFRIEND………………………………	Shayla Lynn Hair
BUBBA……………………………………...	Liam Troncalli
POINDEXTER……………………………….	Erica Romm
BERTHA…………………………………….	Caera Flood, Jenna Getts
SHIRLEY…………………………………….	Maegan Flood
VOCAL COACH……………………………	Tammie Sims
CHOREOGRAPHER……………………….	Sally Ann Weber-Hawthorne
DIRECTOR #1/STAGE MANAGER………	M'Arty Burkart
MOM………………………………………...	Lori Seelig
DAD………………………………………….	Lysle Seelig
SHECKY…………………………………….	Theresa Littlefield
CHANCE/DIRECTOR #2…………………..	Keith Clark
BLANCHE…………………………………..	Jenny Daniel
TRIO & VO ……………………………….	Jenna Getts, Shayla Lynn Hair Caera Flood, Justine Norris
PIANIST…………………………………….	Tim Jenkins

STAFF & THANKS

Frank Steele…………………………	DIRECTOR
Amy Shojai………………………….	MUSIC DIRECTOR
Amy Wallace………………………..	CHOREOGAPHER
Maegan Flood, Shayla Hair…………	ASSISTANT DANCE DESIGN
The Rialto Theater…………………..	LIGHTS/SOUND/TECH
Hope On Houston……………………	REHEARSAL SPACE

ACT 1

Scene 1, MISFIT

The action of the play opens on a bare, dark stage. Actors appear from back of the theater house and enter stage from various positions from audience. WALLY enters first during music intro, a bit tentative, but excited to explore the stage, and watching audience. Each actor or singer enters in time to sing his/her assigned solo until full company takes the stage.

Single spotlight, black stage, each actor hits same mark in turn.

(WALLY)
MY FAMILY DOESN'T GET IT

(BUBBA)
MY GIRLFRIEND DRAGGED ME HERE

(POINDEXTER)
THEY THINK I AM A MISFIT

(WALLY/BUBBA/POINDEXTER)
AND WE AGREE, IT'S CLEAR.

(BERTHA)
PEOPLE THINK I'M DITZY

(SHIRLEY)
MY MOTHER LOVES SHAKESPEARE.
(DIRECTORS)
TOO YOUNG, TOO OLD, TOO BITCHY,
TOO PLAIN, TOO LOUD, TOO TWITCHY,
ECCENTRIC, AND THEY JEER.

(MOM & DAD)
A LITTLE LEFT OF CENTER,
A LITTLE OUT OF TOUCH.
WHEN YOU'RE DIFFERENT
FROM THE OTHERS,
FITTING IN CAN BE
TOO MUCH.

(SHECKY)
MY JOKES ARE MY PROTECTION.

(CHANCE)
MY LOOKS WON'T WIN A CROWN.

(STAGE MANAGER)
BUT MY WEIRD IMPERFECTION
ON STAGE WON'T LET ME DOWN.

(PIANIST)
MAYBE I'M TOO GAWKY,
I'M CHOSEN LAST FOR TEAMS.

(POINDEXTER & SHIRLEY)
TOO SHY FOR STANISLAVSKI,
MY CONFIDENCE IS ROCKY,
BUT THEY DON'T KNOW MY DREAMS.

Full lights up

(ALL)
A LITTLE LEFT OF CENTER,
A LITTLE OUT OF TOUCH,
WHEN YOU'RE DIFFERENT
FROM THE OTHERS.
FITTING IN CAN BE
TOO MUCH.

Single spot, black stage

(LANCE)
EMBRACING STELLA ADLER,
AND SPOLIN IMPROVE GAMES,
A STRASBERG-CHEKHOV ACTOR
LEARNING UTA HAGEN'S NAME.

(WALLY)
MAYBE THEY DON'T GET IT,
AND WE AGREE, IT'S CLEAR.
WITH THEM, I AM A MISFIT,
BUT I'M NORMAL WHEN I'M HERE.

(MOM & DAD)
A LITTLE LEFT OF CENTER,
A LITTLE OUT OF TOUCH.
WHEN YOU'RE DIFF'RENT
FROM THE OTHERS,
FITTING IN CAN BE
TOO MUCH.

MOM & DAD exit.

(DIRECTORS)
A LITTLE LEFT OF CENTER,
A LITTLE OUT OF TOUCH.
WHEN YOU'RE DIFF'RENT
FROM THE OTHERS,
FITTING IN CAN BE
TOO MUCH.

DIRECTORS exit.

Full lights.

(ALL)
MAYBE THEY DON'T GET IT,
AND WE AGREE, IT'S CLEAR.
WITH THEM, I AM A MISFIT,
BUT I'M NORMAL WHEN I'M HERE.

A LITTLE LEFT OF CENTER,
A LITTLE OUT OF TOUCH.

(GIRLS)
WHEN YOU'RE DIFF'RENT

(BOYS)
WHEN YOU'RE DIFF'RENT,

(GIRLS)
FROM THE OTHERS,

(BOYS)
FROM THE OTHERS,

(GIRLS)
FITTING IN,

(BOYS)
FITTING IN,

(ALL)
FITTING IN CAN BE
TOO MUCH.

Scene 2, SLATE

Full lights.

DIR. #1
Cross center stage, take your mark, and slate.

POINDEXTER
(whispers) What do you mean, slate?

CHANCE
Get a load of her, doesn't know what slate means.

DIR. #1
Hit your mark, give your name and agent.

STAGE MANAGER

What's the holdup? Next, already!

POINDEXTER
(crosses center) My name is Sydney Poindexter. *(offstage laughter)* Agent? I guess my mom?

DIR. #1
Thanks, Poindexter. Next. *(beat)* Poindexter, you can leave now.

CHANCE
(swaggers to center) My name is Chandler Von Barrymore. But you can call me Chance. I'm with The Elite Agency.

DIR. #1
Thank you Chance, good to see you again. Next.

SHIRLEY
Mo-om, do I have to?

MOM
For heaven's sake, don't tell them I'm your mother. Go, go, get out there. Sparkle, just like we practice, sparkle. Don't forget to give face.

SHIRLEY
(pause pause) Shirley Ann Temple.

MOM
TempLER!

SHIRLEY
Oh yeah. Templer. And my most special agent is my mom…I mean, Leslie Temple.

MOM
TEMPLER!

DIR. #1
Next.

WALLY
I don't have an agent, I hope that's okay, but I could have an agent if I asked, cuz my cousin's mom's brother Doogie Goforth said I was really good, and I sure wish I had an agent but I'll do the job I promise and and and…. *(blubbering runs off stage, then runs back on, regaining composure)* My name is Wally Carlson. Pleasure to be here, sir.

DIR. #1

Go forth, young man. Next!

BERTHA

(bright, upbeat, cheerleader type) Hi! How are you? My name is Bertha Getts. *(getting serious)* My answer is "World Peace." *(a beat)* Whoops, wrong room. *(pulls out note card, and reads hesitantly from it)*. My agent is Nikolai Armaloupopodis.

DIR. #1

Say again?

BERTHA

Nikolai Armaloupopodis.

STAGE MANAGER

Do you mean Nikolai Armaloupopodis.

BERTHA

I just signed with them! *(runs to place giggling and waving)*

LANCE

(locates director in audience) Uhm, I can do better up here. *(He's all that...strikes a pose well away from designated "mark")* Hello there. Lance. You know. *(starts to go to place)*

DIR. #1

Last name?

LANCE

No, just Lance. *(winks, "shoots" director with finger-gun, and saunters to place)*

SHECKY

Sol Liebowicz but call me Shecky. Two hyenas lying on the plains of Africa. One says to the other, It's awfully hot for a Tuesday. *(only Poindexter laugh—or crickets)*.

DIR. #1

(really loud) NEXT! Please, Next!

BUBBA

(muttering, doesn't want to be there) Bubba Humphrey.

DIR. #1

Louder

                        BUBBA

Bubba Humphrey

                    STAGE MANAGER

What?

                        BUBBA

Bubba Humphrey

> *Various additional actors cross over carrying props that identify themselves as lighting, sound, costumes, props crew. A variety of character types--fat, thin, old, young--walk across stage, crossing, each say name and then take place.*

Scene 3, MY WAY OR THE HIGHWAY

> *Very military, DIRECTOR #1 enters & sings*

CUZ I SAID SO, THAT IS WHY
I'M DIRECTOR AND DICTATOR,
PARTAKER OF ALL THAT'S RIGHT.
CUZ I SAID SO, DON'T YOU CRY
I'M THE BOSS, AND IT'S MY CROSS
THAT I BEAR, AND I CAN'T LOSE SIGHT.

WHEN YOU TRY OUT FOR ME,
WHAT IS IT THAT I'LL SEE?
PERFECTION, DESPERATION,
PERSPIRATION, MAYBE GLEE?
WHEN I CAST, I'D BETTER SEE,
WHAT SUITS ME TO A TEE.
DEDICATION, RESIGNATION,
NO FRUSTRATION, OR JUST FLEE!

(DIR. #1, VOCAL COACH,
CHOREO & STAGE MGR)

IT'S MY SHOW,	
SO STAY OR GO	
IT'S MY RULES,	(ACTORS)
TO PLAY OR NO.	
NO WHINING,	IT'S YOUR SHOW,
DON'T BE PINING	SO STAY OR GO.
FOR SOMETHING	IT'S YOUR RULES,
YOU DON'T KNOW.	TO PLAY OR NO.
I'M THE DIRECTOR,	NO WHINING,
AND DICTATOR,	CAN'T BE PINING
PARTAKER OF	FOR SOMETHING
ALL THAT'S RIGHT.	I DON'T KNOW.
CUZ I SAID SO,	YOU'RE DIRECTOR,
I'M THE BOSS,	AND DICTATOR,
IT'S MY CROSS,	PARTAKER OF
I CAN'T LOSE SIGHT.	ALL THAT'S RIGHT.
SO IT'S MY WAY,	CUZ YOU SAID SO,
ALL THE WAY,	YOU'RE THE BOSS,
OR THE HIGHWAY,	IT'S YOUR CROSS,
YOU CAN'T STAY.	PLEASE DON'T
I DON'T CARE,	LOSE SIGHT.
IF YOU STAY OR GO.	SO IT'S YOUR WAY,
YES IT'S MY WAY,	ALL THE WAY.
ALL THE WAY,	OR THE HIGHWAY,
OR THE HIGHWAY,	AS YOU SAY.
YOU CAN'T STAY.	YOU DON'T CARE
I DON'T CARE,	IF I STAY OR GO.
IF YOU STAY OR GO.	YES IT'S YOUR WAY,
	ALL THE WAY.
	OR THE HIGHWAY,
	AS YOU SAY.
	YOU DON'T CARE
	IF I STAY OR GO.

(ACTORS)

CUZ YOU SAID SO, THAT IS WHY.
YOU'RE DIRECTOR AND DICTATOR,
PARTAKER OF ALL THAT'S RIGHT
CUZ YOU SAID SO, I WON'T CRY.
YOU'RE THE BOSS, AND IT'S MY CROSS
THAT I BEAR, AND I CAN'T LOSE SIGHT.

WHEN I TRY OUT FOR YOU,
WHAT IS IT THAT I'LL DO?
PERFECTION, DESPERATION,
PERSPIRATION, WHAT'S MY CUE?
WHEN I'M CAST, I'D BETTER BE
WHAT SUITS YOU TO A TEE.
DEDICATION, RESIGNATION,
NO FRUSTRATION, NOT FROM ME!

(ACTORS)

IT'S YOUR SHOW,
TO STAY OR GO.
IT'S YOUR RULES,
TO PLAY OR NO.
NOT WHINING,
WON'T BE PINING
TO CHANGE THE
STATUS QUO.
YOU'RE DIRECTOR,
AND DICTATOR,
PARTAKER OF
ALL THAT'S RIGHT.
CUZ YOU SAID SO,
YOU'RE THE BOSS,
IT'S MY CROSS,
I CAN'T LOSE SIGHT!
SO I'LL CHOOSE
ANOTHER WAY.
GOING BROADWAY,
ALL THE WAY.
MAKE YOU BEG
FOR ME NOT TO GO.
YES, IT'S OUR WAY,
ALL THE WAY
GOING BROADWAY,
HERE TO STAY
MAKE YOU BEG
FOR ME NOT TO GO.

(DIRECTORS)

IT'S MY SHOW,
SO STAY OR GO.
IT'S MY RULES,
TO PLAY OR NO.
NO WHINING,
DON'T BE PINING
FOR SOMETHING
YOU DON'T KNOW.
I'M DIRECTOR,
AND DICTATOR,
PARTAKER OF
ALL THAT'S RIGHT.
CUZ I SAID SO,
I'M THE BOSS,
IT'S MY CROSS,
I CAN'T LOSE SIGHT!
YES, IT'S MY WAY,
ALL THE WAY.
OR THE HIGHWAY,
YOU CAN'T STAY
I DON'T CARE
IF YOU STAY, OR GO.
YES, IT'S MY WAY,
ALL THE WAY.
OR THE HIGHWAY,
YOU CAN'T STAY.
I DON'T CARE
IF YOU STAY OR GO.

blackout

SCENE 4, FATHER & SON #1

> *Opens on a bare stage. Father on one side, son on the other, in area lights*

WALLY
(To audience) My name is Percival Wallace Carlson III. Everyone knows me as Wally. I like Wally. It works for me. My father calls me—

DAD
(other side of stage, to audience yells out) Buck!

WALLY
(sighs) Buck. Ya know why? It's manly.

DAD
You're damn right it's manly.

WALLY
(sighs again) My father's known as Percy...not all that manly.

DAD
My uncle called me Buck.

WALLY
Whatever...He wants me to man up. You know...be the macho guy. He fishes, watches every sport on TV, and bowls three nights a week.

DAD
Buck carries a purple book bag. PURPLE! Who does he think he is, Prince? He has a TV in his room, and he watches *Dancing With The Stars*, and those singing shows where someone wins something. Hey...if the winner got a new rod and reel, I might sign up myself.

WALLY
Dad and I have this running thing going over Christmas gifts. Last year, I got a football. I gave him a CD of "Fiddler On The Roof." Two years ago, he gave me the ESPN sports package for my TV. I gave him the complete recordings of George Gershwin. And three years ago--

DAD
I got him a catcher's mitt. A CATCHER'S MIT! And, it was a really nice one, too. He gave me a DVD of "Liza With a Z." I gotta go. *Fishing In The Yukon* is coming on.

WALLY
I gotta go, too. I'm reading *Pippin* and it's at a really good part. See ya later, Dad.

DAD
Yeah, see ya. *(looks around)* Where's my Cabela's cap?

Blackout

SCENE 5, THEATER GAMES #1

Spoken in blackout

LANCE
OK...THEATER GAMES! *Clears throat.* Lights, please! (*Spotlight finally comes on, but in wrong place. LANCE moves into light.*)

LANCE
This promotes getting along, teamwork, and, and, and...getting along. Take the leg of the person next to you. Now, turn a summersault, all the while asking the person whose leg you hold not to make a face. Once you face backward, give the person whose leg you hold a small judo chop to the elbow. Go down the row until each person has been chopped.

Blackout

SCENE 6, SPARKLE

Area lights, both sides of stage, each in own area. SHIRLEY frozen during MOM part of song.

(MOM)
YOU'RE A STAR, BABY,
JUST LIKE ME, BACK IN THE DAY.

I CAN SEE, YOU'LL BE OKAY
JUST AS YOU ARE, JUST AS YOU ARE,
BABY.

LOOK AT THAT FACE, SHE'S MY BABY
MOVING WITH GRACE, LEADING LADY.
SHE CAN DANCE, BELT A NOTE,
WITH ONE GLANCE SEE HER EMOTE.

COULDA BEEN MINE, DON'T MEAN MAYBE,
MY TIME TO SHINE, BABY BABY!
COULD-A BEEN, WITH MY VOICE,
WAY BACK WHEN, I HAD NO CHOICE.

PERFECTION IN REFLECTION,
EACH PRODUCTION HITS THE MARK.
UPON REFLECTING AND PERFECTING,
SHE NEEDS A BIT MORE OF A SPARK!

YES, DIRECTION WITH AFECTION,
EACH CORRECTION WE'LL EMBARK.
WITH MORE PROJECTING, I'M EXPECTING,
AND SHE WILL SHINE BRIGHT IN THE DARK!

SPARKLE!
GO AHEAD, SPARKLE!
BAT YOUR EYES,
TURN AND SPIN,
GIVE 'EM SOMETHING NEW.

SPARKLE!
TRUST ME AND SPARKLE!
FEED THE CROWD
THAT'S LOVING YOU.
STOP THE SIGHS
AND JUST BEGIN.

SHIRLEY unfreezes, each still sing more to audience than each other.

(SHIRLEY)	(MOM)
SPARKLE IS ALL THAT I HEAR	SPARKLE!
AND IT'S NOT MUSIC TO MY EAR,	GO AHEAD, SPARKLE!

IT'S A WORD THAT I FEAR,

PLEASE DON'T SAY IT!

I DO THE BEST THAT I CAN
WHY CAN'T YOU PLEASE.
UNDERSTAND
THAT'S A WORD I'D LIKE TO BAN,

PLEASE DON'T SAY IT.

YOUR DREAM JUST
ISN'T MINE.
I RESPECT YOU,
AND IT'S FINE.
CAN I PLEASE GIVE YOU
SOME NEW SIGN?
JUST SO THAT WORD,
NO! PLEASE DON'T SAY.

MY ACTING JUST AIN'T,
ISN'T PEARLS.
NOT LIKE THOSE
OTHER GIRLS
WHO GRACE THE STAGE WITH
ALL THEIR TWIRLS.
I ASK AGAIN,
DON'T SAY THAT WORD!

SPARKLE!

SHE ALWAYS SPARKLES!

SHE CAN DANCE,
BELT A NOTE
WITH ONE GLANCE
SEE HER EMOTE.

SPARKLE!

HOW CAN I BE
BE LIKE MY MUSE?
SHOOTING STAR
FALLS TOO FAR,
NEVER FEAR,
I'LL HOLD YOU, DEAR.

BAT YOUR EYES,
TURN AND SPIN
THAT'S THE WAY
TO SHOW…
SPARKLE!
TRUST ME AND
SPARKLE!
WATCH ME BABY SO
YOU'LL KNOW.
NEVER EVER QUIT.

LOOK AT THAT FACE,
THERE'S NO MAYBE,
HEAR THAT VOICE,
LEADING LADY.
HIT YOUR MARK,
BOW AND GRIN.
DO IT LIKE A PRO.

WHAT ABOUT ME?
PAID MY DUES.
GO AHEAD,
SPARKLE!
SHOOTING STAR
FALLS TOO FAR
NEVER FEAR,
I'LL HOLD YOU DEAR.

MOM and SHIRLY to each other

	PERFECTION IN REFLECTION,
EACH PRODUCTION HITS THE MARK.	
	UPON REFLECTING AND PERFECTING,
WE NEED A BIT MORE OF A SPARK.	
	YES, DIRECTION WITH AFFECTION,
EACH CORRECTION WE'LL EMBARK. WITH MORE PROJECTING I'M EXPECTING MAYBE I'LL SHINE BRIGHT IN THE DARK.	EACH CORRECTION WE'LL EMBARK WITH MORE PROJECTING I'M EXPECTING I KNOW SHE'LL SHINE BRIGHT IN THE DARK.
	Nine bars instrumental before they come together and sing to end.
OKAY, I'LL SPARKLE! MOMMA, DON'T BE SO MATRIARCHAL.	SPARKLE! GO AHEAD, SPARKLE! THAT'S A WORD THAT I FEAR, PLEASE DON'T SAY IT!
I DO THE BEST THAT I CAN DON'T YOU KNOW I'M YOUR BIGGEST FAN?	SPARKLE! TRUST ME AND SPARKLE! IT'S YOUR TIME. . .
WE BOTH CAN SHINE. TRUST ME MOMMA.	
YOU WILL BE A STAR!	TRUST ME BABY, YOU WILL BE A STAR!

Blackout

SCENE 7, KNOW IT ALL #1

Spotlight comes on. LANCE on mark, but spot to one side. LANCE moves into light—and light moves. He finally gets into light.

LANCE
(*reading from note card*) I just got a question from Stockholm, Sweden from a mister Biorn Knudtsun. He asks, "Just how long ago did really good comedy writing for the stage and screen begin?"

Well, Tom, I'm glad you asked that one. Believe it or not, the first and best of the Swiss comedy writers was General George Armstrong Custer. His book, <u>Predicting Rain On The Prairie</u> was a huge hit. Oh, and once I saw a porcupine!

LANCE exits, but SPOT stays on. He sees it's still on, dashes back onstage to get back into light—and it goes out just as he arrives.

Scene 8, PIANO MAN

On dark stage, in spotlight, noodling on piano… monologue with offstage voices.

PIANIST
Why people love me, why they should fear me, I'm the glue that holds everything together…
    I started piano lessons when I was 5. You'd never know it now, but I had to work really hard at it—my folks just thought it was something to

pass the time. Bu you see, it really mattered to me. To do it right. To be really good at something.

I'm not there yet, but still trying.

Do you recognize this song? Of course not. It's an original. I don't get many chances to play my own stuff.

I figure I've played (*plays ~30 second riff of TOMORROW from Annie*), 2126 times, but who's counting? And I smile, and I nod, and I play, and I watch every kid in town with a brand new red wig try to sing it. And tomorrow never comes.

Don't get me wrong, I love what I do. But every once in a while a musician needs a rest. Get it? Oh never mind.

DIRECTOR #1

Hey [name] we need you to stay late. And the song's too high for [name] so could you write it down a couple steps? Thanks!

PIANIST

(*he plays heavy handed TOMORROW but in minor key*) Here's what you might not understand. I play in the orchestra, but also for every rehearsal. The solos usually are fine, because I get to play the written accompaniment. But the chorus rehearsals can fall flat. Get it? Okay, never mind.

See, the chorus stuff has lots of lines to learn, sometimes with singers who don't read music, or can't reach the notes. So who gets to play all the parts in a new order? (*celebration chord—a "ta-da" D-major*)

CHOREOGRAPHER

Hey [name] the dance needs to go faster, a LOT faster!

PIANIST

That's right. It's the dance stuff, too. (*plays TOMORROW really fast*)

CHOREOGRAPHER

Yeah, go faster on that part.

PIANIST

Which part?

CHOREOGRAPHER

You know, that part that's in that deal. That thing we were going over the other night. It was something about, I don't know, I don't remember, but you know, that part. That should be faster.

PIANIST

(*under his breath*) Not exactly a Julliard graduate.

MOM
My daughter worked two years at Casa Manana . . .

PIANIST
(*under breath*) probably with lines like, "Milk Duds are 50-cents, and the large box is 75-cents. Would you care for a cold drink?"

MOM
Your introduction to her song must be SPECIAL, to show case her extraordinary voice.

PIANIST
(plays the worms crawl in the works crawl out...) Oh, and here comes the vocal coach. S/he at least understands music. Mostly. I've worked with some great vocal coaches. And then some that—

VOCAL COACH
You're playing too LOUD. Except at measure 297, and the pick up to 586 is too fast, and I want the adagio faster, and play song #12 sort of…you know…slithery.

PIANIST
(plays TOMORROW like a march) Something else you may not know. People like me, we're rarely paid, unless you get to the pro level. Like I said, I started taking lessons when I was five, so that means I've been playing [how many years]. Pianists may have full time jobs, maybe teaching, or rushing from playing for the church to get to a matinee performance on time. Going to class during the day getting a degree. Or taking care of our own kids. And if we get sick well, the show must go on. There's no understudy for the piano player. Sure, they've got those audio recording tracks now and they work great for some rehearsals but for me—nothing beats live music.

SINGER
Hey man, wanted to thank you for saving my bacon. Don't know how I missed that entrance, but the audience never knew—it was seamless. You're a lifesaver, a true pro!

PIANIST
(long pause) A recording couldn't do that. And you wonder why I do this? Enough said.

SCENE 9, BOOGIE WOOGIE LAFFS

Full lights, works the stage & audience

(SHECKY)
WELL, I'M REALLY STEADY FREDDY,
GOT A JOKE AT THE READY,
GONNA GET A BIG LAUGH OR SMILE.
FIVE'LL GETCHA FIFTY,
GONNA THINK I'M KINDA NIFTY,
GONNA MAKE YA LAUGH QUITE A WHILE.

MAN IT'S WHAT I DO.
I DO THE FUNNY THROUGH AND THROUGH.
I'M SHARING MY WIT WITH YOU.
YOU'RE GONNA LOVE IT!

SINCE I'M TRULY FUNNY FRED,
I'LL WEAR A BOXER OR A TEDDY,
ANYTHING TO GET A GRIN.
MY STYLE IS KINDA HOT,
YA MIGHT LIKE IT, MAYBE NOT,
GONNA HIT THE COMIC SPIN.

MAN, IT'S WHAT I DO.
I DO THE FUNNY THROUGH AND THROUGH.
I'M GONNA BE A HIT WITH YOU.
YOU'RE GONNA LOVE IT.

Background music behind talking chorus break

I feed my cow sawdust instead of hay. The milk tastes OK, but I'm pretty tired of drinking the splinters. (*offstage RIMSHOT*)

A preacher tells his flock, "Take all of the whisky bottles in your house and throw them in the river. Take all of the whisky bottles on your street, and throw them in the river. Take all of the whisky bottles in the town and throw them in the river. Now, let us all sing, 'Shall We Gather At The River.' " *(RIMSHOT)*

HEY THERE, PRETTY BETTY,
SINCE YOU KNOW ME, CLEVER FREDDY,
DOES MY COMEDY WORK FOR YOU?
GOT A MILLION JOKES,
I'LL EVEN TRY 'EM ON YOUR FOLKS.
SOME ARE KINDA OLD, SOME NEW.

MAN, IT'S WHAT I DO.
I DO THE FUNNY THROUGH AND THROUGH.
I'LL DO A BIT FOR YOU.
YOU'RE GONNA LOVE IT.

SINCE I'M DANG FUNNY FREDDY,
AND MY JOKES ARE KINDA HEADY,
ALL I GOTTA DO IS SPEAK.
I KINDA LIKE TO SAY
THAT MY STUFF'S ABOUT TODAY,
MAYBE NOT FOR THE MEEK.

MAN, IT'S WHAT I DO.
I DO THE FUNNY THROUGH AND THROUGH.
I'M ON FIRE AND LIT FOR YOU.
YOU'RE GONNA LOVE IT.

Background music behind talking chorus break

A ventriloquist and his dummy walk into a bar. Bar tender says, "What'll you have?" Ventriloquist says, "I'll have a double ginger ale, but I can't speak for the other guy." *(RIMSHOT)*

A man walks into a shoe store and asks, "Do you have alligator shoes?" The clerk says, "Well, bring your alligator in and we'll try to fit him." *(RIMSHOT)*

MAN, IT'S WHAT I DO.
I DO THE FUNNY THROUGH AND THROUGH.
I'LL TELL A JOKE AND SIT WITH YOU.
YOU'RE GONNA LOVE IT!

blackout

SCENE 10, KNOW IT ALL ACTOR #2

Spotlight—LANCE walks into light

LANCE
I have a question from Irving Goldberg from Miami, Florida. He asks, "I love Dixieland music. Is it an American art form?"

Well, Danny, I get that one a lot. Sure, the harpsichord is used primarily in the kind of music you mention, but don't underestimate what being trained by a professional actor can do for your career. *Spotlight goes out. LANCE speaks last line with exasperation.* I hope this helped you. *(stage whisper to LIGHTS)* You did that on purpose!

SCENE 11, I'M IN IT FOR THE BABES

This is a jazzy big band splashy song for a nerdy guy and a girl trio. It's a transformation song from nerd to confidant guy.

Area light on CHANCE in opening. Spoken under soft piano music...

CHANCE
Look at me. Look at me...look. What do you see? I used to watch guys dating, guys having fun, couples...lots of couples. I had nothing. I'm not handsome. Not witty. Not what girls wanted.

 Then...I discovered "it." "It" being show biz. SHOW BIZ! All of a sudden, I had purpose. I discovered that I could do things that none of the other guys could do. I could become whatever I wanted to be...whatever a part called for.

 And, the girls? Well, I've got to admit. It has benefits...HIT IT!

FULL LIGHTS, Big, loud music

(CHANCE)
I'M IN IT.

(GIRL TRIO)
YES, HE'S IN IT

(CHANCE)
FOR THE BABES,
AND THE BABES ARE GETTIN' INTO ME.

(GIRL TRIO)
HE'S IN IT

(CHANCE)
YES, I'M IN IT.

(GIRL TRIO)
WATCH HIM GO,
GOSH, OH GOLLY,
OH GEE.

(CHANCE)
I CAN ACT. I CAN DANCE.
I CAN REALLY SING.
I CAN BOP. I CAN WALTZ.
I CAN DO THE SWING.
I CAN BLACK BOTTOM, CHARLESTON,
AND BUCK AND WING.
PREPARE TO BE DAZZLED
WHEN I DO MY THING.
I'M IN IT FOR THE BABES!

(GIRL TRIO-JAZZ TALK)
FLIPPILDY, RIPPILDY,
RICKITY ROOVE.
WE GET ALL EXCITED WHEN WE
WATCH HIM MOVE.
NEVER SAW ANYONE IN
SUCH A GROOVE.
HE DOESN'T HAVE ANYTHING
LEFT TO PROVE.
HE'S IN IT FOR THE BABES!

(CHANCE)
I'M IN IT

(GIRL TRIO)
YES, HE'S IN IT.

(CHANCE)
FOR THE BABES,
CUZ THE BABES LIKE WHAT I DO.

(GIRL TRIO)
HE'S IN IT.

(CHANCE)
YES, I'M IN IT.

(GIRL TRIO)
WATCH HIM WORK,
HECK, MY GOODNESS,
IT'S TRUE.

(CHANCE)
I CAN ACT, WHEN I DO IT
BRINGS A TEAR.
IT CAN BRING A SMILE,
OR A LITTLE FEAR.
SHAKESPEARE, IBSEN,
BRING THEM ON.
MIGHT SCARE ME A LITTLE,
BUT IT WON'T LAST LONG.
I'M IN IT FOR THE BABES.

(GIRL TRIO-JAZZ TALK)
HOP, BOP, BOOG, TOP
WATCH HIM EMOTE.
THOSE KIND OF SKILLS,
I'LL SURE PROMOTE.
HEARD HIM HIT THE TOP OF A
MUSICAL NOTE.
HE'LL EVEN BE FAMOUS
IN TERRE HAUTE.
HE'S IN IT FOR THE BABES!

25 Bar DANCE BREAK

(GIRL TRIO)
YOU'RE IN IT.

(CHANCE)
YES, I'M IN IT

(GIRL TRIO)
FOR THE BABES,
AND WE'RE GOING CRAZY FOR YOU.

(CHANCE)
I'M IN IT.

(GIRL TRIO)
YES, YOU'RE IN IT.

(CHANCE)
ALL I CAN SAY IT'S
WHAT I WAS MEANT TO DO.

(GIRL TRIO)
YOU CAN OUT SING SINATRA.
YOU CAN OUT DANCE FRED.
YOUR ACTING PUTS OLIVIER
ON HIS HEAD.
YOU CAN LAUGH, YOU CAN SMILE,
YOU CAN CRY ON CUE.
THERE'S JUST NOTHING LEFT
THAT YOU CAN'T DO.
YOU'VE MADE IT WITH THE BABES!

(ALL-JAZZ TALK)
FLIP, FLOP, BIP, BOP,
WATCH US SWING.
JAZZ, THE SLIDE, JUST
ANY OLD THING.
DISCO, TAP, AND
MODERN, TOO.
EVEN BALLET, IF I
HAVE THE RIGHT SHOE.
NOW, THE ACTING, THE SINGING,

AND THE DANCING IS THROUGH.
HOW ABOUT WE SING OUR LAST
VERSE FOR YOU!

(ALL SING)
WE'RE IN IT.
YES, WE'RE IN IT.
FOR THE SHOW,
CUZ SHOW BIZ
GRABBED AHOLD OF US.

WE'RE IN IT.
YES, WE'RE IN IT.
IT WILL BE MY LIFE,
DON'T GO
KICKIN' UP A FUSS.

WE'RE OUR OWN STAGE MOMS,
WE KNOW WHAT WE NEED.
CAN'T WAIT TO GET STARTED,
HAFTA PICK UP SPEED.
I'LL HIT THE STAGE
WITH A MIGHTY FORCE.
AM I THAT GOOD?
WELL, SURE, OF COURSE.
WANT GREAT SHOW-BIZ,
WELL I'M THE SOURCE.

(CHANCE)
I THINK I'VE MADE IT!

(GIRL TRIO)
YES, HE'S MADE IT!

(ALL)
WE'VE ALL MADE IT...
MADE IT
WITH THE SHOW!

Blackout

SCENE 12, KNOW IT ALL ACTOR #3

Two area lights, LANCE confused but chooses one light. It goes out. Throws up hands, moves to other one.

LANCE
I love this one. It's from Marty Snookfield in Amarillo, Texas. He writes, "You don't hear much about Laurel and Hardy these days. Are they still alive and active in movies?"

Murray, I get this one every day. They're very much alive and well. When movies changed, they both retired and took jobs as roadies for Twisted Sister. (*Light goes out, other one goes on and he must move.*) In fact, and a lot of people don't know this, stock car racing is bigger today than it was even a hundred and fifty years ago. (*exits*)

SCENE 13, WE'RE NOT BABIES!

Full lights up

STAGE MANAGER
(*Watches LANCE leave.*) What a stage hog!

BUBBA
Yeah, he's good.

POINDEXTER
Stage hog? That's rude, he doesn't eat that much!

STAGE MANAGER
Oh yes he does, he chews the scenery. Gobbles up everyone's ambition on stage. With all the trouble we've had with cutting funding for the arts, why couldn't they include "stage hog" in those cuts.

CHANCE

Gosh, but he really is good. And what's so wrong about showing off? Isn't that what it's all about?

BERTHA
I've seen it before. They start out insecure but talented, and then the applause feeds the ego, and they morph into a scene stealer. Instead of the show, it becomes all about THEM.

STAGE MANAGER
There's a cure for it, you know.

CHANCE
(Looks worried.) Push 'em off the stage? You know, I didn't mean to bump into you during that last song . . .

POINDEXTER
I heard about an actor one time, hacked off the costumer and ended up with pins in the wrong places, if you know what I mean.

BERTHA
Yep, and the music director can speed up a song so you want to curl up and die. Not that it's happened to me, of course.

STAGE MANAGER
Suck it up, sweetheart. There's no crying in acting. Unless it's in the script.

BERTHA
Wonder how you cry on stage, on cue?

CHANCE
I've seen actors cry at auditions. Especially when they don't get cast.

BUBBA
Crying's the easiest thing in the world. All you have to do is at the right time, reach into your nose and pull out some hairs.

BERTHA
Ewww. Does that work?

BUBBA
Sure it does. That's how I got my parents to buy me my first car.

STAGE MANAGER
What a baby!

ALL ACTORS TOGETHER
We're not babies!

POINDEXTER
And I'm tired of being told I'm too young for the part. Or for the script.

BERTHA
Yeah, and tired of the adults sanitizing scripts for our dainty ears.

WALLY
And telling us we don't have the experience to understand. Quit protecting us! Theater reflects real life. Believe me, we've heard worse.

POINDEXTER
Some of us have lived worse. (*Everyone pauses, takes a beat.*) Sometimes, I just want the chance to try. Even if I don't get to be the star.

STAGE MANAGER
Yeah? (*Gives her a hug.*) Well, it's not all about being a star.

SCENE 14, STARZ

> *COMPANY enters, taking their places and poses around stage during BERTHA monologue. DAD watches impatiently.*

BERTHA

Look at all these Thespians. We all come to the Theater in different ways, and for different reasons. He came to get a date…and stayed. She's here because of her mom. They're here because they love making techie magic. And maybe some are here to be (*air quotes*) STARS.

A star is the flavor of the month, popular with directors and audiences for an eye blink, desperate to hang on to what was. Actors work forever, reinvent themselves to stay current and embrace all the flaws that make them who they are, and what they will be. Even the failures matter—everything is material. You just can't quit.

Three area lights, BERTHA center, MOM & SHIRLEY and WALLY & DAD on each side of stage.

(BERTHA to AUDIENCE)
IT'S ONLY MAKE BELIEVE.
IT'S ONLY MAKE BELIEVE.
THE GROWNUPS ALL PERCEIVE,
IT'S SIMPLE LIES WE WEAVE,
WE'RE PLAYING WITH THE FACTS.

IT'S ONLY MAKE BELIEVE.
THEY THINK IT'S MAKE BELIEVE.
A CHILDREN'S GAME THAT'S FAKE.
THERE'S SO MUCH MORE AT STAKE.
FOR US, IT'S NOT AN ACT.

(MOM singing to SHIRLEY)
A LITTLE LEFT OF CENTER,
A LITTLE OUT OF TOUCH.
WHEN YOU'RE DIFF'RENT,
FROM THE OTHERS,
FITTING IN CAN BE
TOO MUCH.

(WALLY singing to DAD)
THEY SAY, "DON'T BE NAÏVE,
IT'S ONLY MAKE BELIEVE."
PERFORMERS ALL CONCEIVE,
OUR GIFTS ARE WHAT WE LEAVE,
AND WE WILL HAVE YOUR BACK.

WHEN AUDIENCE BELIEVES,
THEY'RE GIVEN A REPRIEVE.
THERE'S TRUTH IN EV'RY STORY,
AND THAT'S THE SIMPLE GLORY,
ALLOWING ALL TO FEEL.

(MOM)
WE CRY FOR YOU, SIGH FOR YOU,
LAUGH, HURT AND LIE FOR YOU.
TRY TO GET BY, AND YES,
SOMETIMES WE DIE.

(WALLY)
A MIRROR REFLECTION

IS JUST WHAT WE GIVE . . .
REVEALING THE REASONS
WHY ALL OF US LIVE!

(BERTHA)
IT'S NOT ABOUT THE BEING,
BUT RATHER ALL THE REACHING
TO THE STARZ.

IT'S NOT ABOUT ARRIVING
BUT EVERYONE WHO'S STRIVING
FOR THE STARZ! TO THE STARZ!

(MOM)
FOREVER PERFECTING
THE CRAFT WE ARE MAKING
THE TALENT WE BRING
THAT COMPOSES THE DREAM

(BERTHA)
TOGETHER, WE'RE BETTER,
BE GENEROUS, FRIEND.
NO SOLO IS SOLO
WHEN ALL OF US WIN!

All lights up.

(COMPANY)
IT'S NOT ABOUT THE BEING,
BUT RATHER ALL THE REACHING
TO THE STARZ! TO THE STARZ!

IT'S NOT ABOUT ARRIVING
BUT E'VRY ONE WHO'S STRIVING
FOR THE STARZ! FOR THE STARZ!
FOR THE STARZ!

WALLY, DADY, SHIRLEY and MOM remain on stage as rest of cast exits.

SCENE 15, MAKE ME PROUD

> *DAD motions WALLY over, MOM and SHIRLEY eavesdrop from other side of stage.*

WALLY
(*Joins DAD.*) What are you doing here?

DAD
Why are you wasting your time with this? I got two tickets on the 50 yard line for the big game.

WALLY
Dad, I already told you I have rehearsal. And it's not a waste of time.

DAD
But it's just a rehearsal. Tonight's the game.

WALLY
Bet the players practice just as much as I rehearse, is that a waste of time? And I need all the practice I can get. I'm not a natural like they are. (*indicates SHIRLEY and MOM*)

DAD
An actor is an actor. You're either an actor or you're not an actor. Rehearsals don't matter. Now these guys playing football, that takes rehearsal.

WALLY
It's called practice, Dad. (*a beat*) So you're saying no matter how hard I try, I'm not going to make it?

DAD
I don't want you to embarrass yourself.

WALLY
Embarrass myself, or embarrass you? I know I'm not what you wanted in a son, and calling me Buck doesn't change who I am.

DAD
But calling you Buck might save a lot of embarrassment for you. Why can't you be "Buck?" Just once, try being Buck. If you're such a great actor, it shouldn't be a stretch.

WALLY
But I'm not a great actor. That's why I rehearse. Can't you try, just once, to be proud of me for who I am?

DAD
The game starts in 20 minutes. C'mon Buck, please go with me.

WALLY
Why is this so important? It's just a game, and it's not even your favorite team.

DAD
(*beat*) I don't want you to go through what I went through. I was a scrawny kid. I was the weakling. I was the kid they joked about on the beach that got sand kicked in his face. But I made myself change. I did everything my father wanted me to do. He hunted, he fished, he did every macho thing every father did, in those days. Know what I really wanted to do. (*looks embarrassed*) I wanted to write poetry. That's it, I just wanted to write poetry. I never told my dad.

WALLY
Then you have to understand how I feel about theater. Is it better to risk embarrassment for a moment, or live a lifetime of regret? Be disappointed forever, wondering what might have been? If I fail, at least I'll know.

DAD
(*angry*) I'm trying to protect you! You're my son, I don't want you hurt.

WALLY
Are you trying to protect me, or protect you? I know what your friends think.

DAD
Can you just be Buck, for once, and go to the game with me? Yes or no?

WALLY
Find someone else to use your extra ticket, dad.

WALLY joins MOM and SHIRLEY on other side of stage. DAD stares at the tickets in his hand.

SHIRLEY
(*excited*) I heard your Dad got tickets to the big game! Aren't you going?

WALLY

We've got rehearsal.

SHIRLEY

But it's only one rehearsal. If you're not going, can I go?

MOM

No, you need the practice. I don't want you to embarrass yourself.

SHIRLEY

Embarrass myself, or embarrass you? Not everyone loves the spotlight, and backstage stuff is just as important, you know. I'm not what you wanted in a daughter, and calling me Shirley Temple doesn't change who I am. (*exits*)

MOM

Templer! (*MOM and WALLY exit, leaving DAD alone on stage*).

Flashing lights, maybe fireworks

(DAD)

MAKE ME PROUD, BY GOLLY
MAKE ME PROUD—
ON THE FIELD OF PLAY
YELL IT GOOD AND LOUD.
GONNA SPIKE THAT BALL,
SUMMER, SPRING OR FALL,
MAKE ME PROUD, BY GOLLY,
ALWAYS MAKE ME PROUD . . .

(soft music, soft area light)

(*speaking*) Do I mean that? Sure, I do. I think I do. I want to . . . But my son (*softly*), my son . . .

MAKE ME KNOW YOU, MY BOY
HAVE ME KNOW YOU, MY BOY
LET'S FORGET ALL THE STRIFE,
YOU'RE THE WHOLE OF MY LIFE.
HOW SHOULD I KNOW YOU, MY BOY?
CAN I KNOW YOU, MY BOY?
DO I KNOW YOU, MY BOY?
THESE FEELINGS CUT LIKE A KNIFE.
YOU'RE THE WHOLE OF MY LIFE.
HOW SHOULD I KNOW YOU, MY BOY?

I SAW YOU AS ME,
NOT YOU AS YOU.
AN EXTENSION OF ME.
AND I NEVER ASKED "WHO."

HELP ME, MY BOY,
PLEASE, HELP ME KNOW.
I'M STUBBORN AT TIMES,
PERHAPS A BIT SLOW.

Music interlude—soft area light up on WALLY other side of stage in rehearsal pose, lights down on WALLY as DAD sings again.

THESE FEELINGS CUT LIKE A KNIFE.
YOU'RE THE WHOLE OF MY LIFE.
HOW SHOULD I KNOW YOU, MY BOY?

HELP ME TO KNOW YOU, MY BOY.
LET ME TO KNOW YOU, MY BOY.
SURELY WE'LL GET THERE, MY SON,
AT THE SPEED OF A RUN.

WE'LL GET THERE, I SAY
MAYBE SOON, OR SOMEDAY.
I'LL SAY IT OUT LOUD,
THAT'S MY BOY! YES, I'M PROUD.

(quietly spoken) My son.

Slow blackout

SCENE 16, TALK DIRTY TO ME

> *The BEEP-sound is a bicycle bulb horn STAGE MANAGER honks to cover up bad word. Full lights.*

CASTING DIRECTOR
Slate.

BUBBA
(To director in audience.) Do I really have to read this?

CASTING DIRECTOR
Please Slate.

BUBBA
Bubba Humphrey.

CASTING DIRECTOR
This is a make or break part. Whenever you're ready, Mr. Humphrey. I'll feed you the lines.

BUBBA
Ready when you are.

CASTING DIRECTOR
From page 16. "I want you out of here right now."

BUBBA
Don't tell me what to do, you son of a BEEP. Who in the BEEP do you think you are? I don't have to take BEEP from some BEEP- hole like you. Step outside, and I'll kick your BEEP.

CASTING DIRECTOR
What page are you reading from Mr. Humphrey?

BUBBA
Page 61.

CASTING DIRECTOR
No, I said 16. You're reading for the preacher.

BUBBA
I'm so sorry, I'm so embarrassed.

CASTING DIRECTOR
No problem. Try the preacher, on page 16. I'll feed you the line again. . .

BUBBA
But why in the BEEP didn't you stop me?

CASTING DIRECTOR
Next!

Blackout

Scene 17, BROKEN DREAMS

Spotlight

DIRECTOR #2
What do you do when the dream is broken? Can dreams be broken? Is it time to go away, is it time to pack things in? Should you try for just one more day? I knocked on the show business door for years. Sometimes they opened it just a crack, enough to get a glimpse, but I could never get all the way in. When I was fat, thin people were in. When I lost weight, all they wanted were fat people. I spent years working on accents, going from agent to agent, taking dance (I hate dance, still can't do it), and arguing with vocal coaches whether to character my way through a song or go opera on 'em.

I can sell a song if I have to. I can act with the best of them. And I can cry on cue. But somehow, that's not enough.

I'm through. I've had it. Isn't thirty-five years enough to devote to something? Just because you love something doesn't mean it has to love you back. I'm sad, but it's time to face reality. I'm calling my agent and telling her I'm through. (*phone rings*) Could that be my agent? Naw, I'm done. I mean, it could be my agent. But why bother. I won't fit the suit anyway.

But wait. What if the suit fits me? For once? I'm going to answer. And pray that this is the one. God, please make it the one.

(*picks up phone, very quietly*) Hello?

Blackout

Scene 18, FIT THE SUIT

Costumer with tape measure and clothes, holding up to check fitting on various actors. Four actor/soloists introduce the song, then joined by entire company.

Four area lights, each soloist lit during their part only.

          (SOPRANO)

INGENUE, GIVE ME
SOMETHING NEW
IT'S NOT OK
THEY CAST ME
THIS WAY.

          (TENOR)

CHARACTER
I WANT
LAUGHTER
IN EVERY LINE
SO I CAN SHINE

          (ALTO)

PIROUETTE,
ENOUGH
WITH SWEAT!
TAP, JAZZ OR SWING,
NO! I WANT TO SING.

          (BASS)

BARITONE,
CAN'T I
CHANGE MY TONE?
SO LONG TO SONG
A CHANGE CAN'T BE WRONG.

Full lights

                    (ALL)

DONCHA KNOW, KNOW,
FOR EVERY SHOW, SHOW,
FOR EVERY SHOW, SHOW,
YA GOTTA FIT THE SUIT?

TALL AS THAT, THAT,
SHORT OR FAT, FAT,
FOR EVERY SHOW, SHOW,
YA GOTTA FIT THE SUIT!

IT'S A RULE
THEY NEVER TELL IT,
BUT WHEN YER COOL
FOREVER SELL IT!

BLACK OR GREEN, GREEN,
IT DON'T MEAN A THING, THING,
FOR EVERY SHOW, SHOW,
YOU GOTTA FIT THE SUIT.

                    (SOPRANOS)

DONCHA KNOW, KNOW,
FOR EVERY SHOW, SHOW,
YES, EVERY SHOW, SHOW,
YA GOTTA FIT THE SUIT.

                    (TENORS)

TALL AS THAT, THAT,
SHORT OR FAT, FAT,
FOR EVERY SHOW, SHOW,
YA GOTTA FIT THE SUIT.

                    (ALTOS & BASSES)

IT'S A RULE
THEY NEVER TELL IT.
BUT WHEN YOU'RE COOL
FOREVER SELL IT!

Sung in a "round." Sops begins alone, each part comes in following previous part.

(SOP)	(TENOR)	(ALTO)	(BASS)
INGENUE GIVE ME SOMETHING NEW IT'S NOT OK THEY CAST ME THIS WAY.	CHARACTER I WANT LAUGHTER IN EVERY LINE SO I CAN SHINE	PIROUETTE, ENOUGH WITH SWEAT! TAP, JAZZ OR SWING, NO! I WANT TO SING.	BARITONE, CAN'T I CHANGE MY TONE? SO LONG TO SONG A CHANGE CAN'T BE WRONG.

(SOPRANOS & ALTOS)
DONCHA KNOW, KNOW,
FOR EVERY SHOW, SHOW,
FOR EVERY SHOW, SHOW,
YA GOTTA FIT THE SUIT?

(TENORS & BASSES)
TALL AS THAT, THAT,
SHORT OR FAT, FAT,
FOR EVERY SHOW, SHOW,
YA GOTTA FIT THE SUIT!

(SOPRANOS & ALTOS)
IT'S A RULE
THEY NEVER TELL IT,

(TENORS & BASSES)
BUT WHEN YER COOL
FOREVER SELL IT!

(ALL)
BLACK OR GREEN, GREEN,
IT DON'T MEAN A THING, THING,
FOR EVERY SHOW, SHOW,
YA GOTTA FIT THE SUIT.

(TENORS & BASES)
DONCHA KNOW, KNOW,
FOR EVERY SHOW, SHOW,
FOR EVERY SHOW, SHOW,
YA GOTTA FIT THE SUIT?

(SOPRANOS & ALTOS)
TALL AS THAT, THAT,
SHORT OR FAT, FAT,
FOR EVERY SHOW, SHOW,
YA GOTTA FIT THE SUIT!

(TENORS & BASSES)
IT'S A RULE
THEY NEVER TELL IT,

(SOPRANOS & ALTOS)
BUT WHEN YER COOL
FOREVER SELL IT!

(ALL)
BLACK OR GREEN, GREEN,
IT DON'T MEAN A THING, THING,
FOR EVERY SHOW, SHOW,
YA GOTTA FIT THE SUIT.

(BASSES)
I WANT DRAMA TODAY

(TENORS)
IN A NEW WAY!

(ALTOS)
NO MORE BALLET!

(SOPRANOS)
IN EV'RY PLAY!

(ALL)
YA KNOW, KNOW!
GOTTA FIT THE SUIT!

Blackout

INTERMISSION

ACT 2

Scene 1, DREAMS NEVER DIE

Spotlight on soloist center stage, as music begins.

(DIRECTOR 2)
I GOT TO TRY JUST ONE MORE DAY.
CAN'T SAY GOODBYE, WON'T GO AWAY.
IT'S WHO I AM, IT'S WHAT I DO.
PLEASE LOVE ME BACK, CUZ I LOVE YOU.

I JUST CAN'T LIE, CAN ONLY SAY
HOW HARD I TRY, MY DUES I PAY
IT'S WHO I AM, IT'S WHAT I DO
PLEASE LOVE ME BACK, CUZ I LOVE YOU.

YOUR PROMISE IS BROKEN
WHEN HOPES GO UNSPOKEN,
A TRAGEDY SEASONED WITH
WHAT-IFS AND TEARS.

COMPASSION INVOKING,
EACH PASSION PROVOKING.
A COMEDY PLAYED DESPITE
MY SECRET FEARS.

CAN'T CHANGE MY HEART, WHAT E'ER I LACK,
I PLAY MY PART! PLEASE LOVE ME BACK.
IT'S WHAT I DO, I'M NOT A SHAM.
CUZ I LOVE YOU, WITH ALL I AM.

YOUR PROMISE IS BROKEN
WHEN HOPES GO UNSPOKEN
A TRAGEDY SEASONED WITH
WHAT-IFS AND TEARS.

COMPASSION INVOKING,
EACH PASSION PROVOKING
A COMEDY PLAYED DESPITE
MY SECRET FEARS.

DON'T BREAK MY HEART AGAIN TODAY.
PLEASE DON'T DEPART, DON'T GO AWAY.
IT'S WHO I AM, DREAMS NEVER DIE,
HOWEVER LONG THE DREAMERS TRY.
HOWEVER LONG THE DREAMERS TRY.

Blackout

SCENE 2, I'M PERFECT

Full lights

UNISON
I'm perfect. They're not. (*pointing at each other*)

MOM
Look at her: beautiful hair, gorgeous eyes, and get a load of this profile. (*gestures to SHIRLEY*)

BUBBA
Look at me: beautiful hair, gorgeous eyes, and get a load of this profile. (*strikes pose to side*)

SHECKY
(*gets in between them, belches loudly*) And get a load of me. After I burped, all you're thinking about is me.

MOM
She's poetry in motion—comes from years of ballet and jazz. (*SHIRLEY dances a few steps*)

BUBBA
Ladies swoon when I enter a room—comes from years of body sculpting--

SHECKY
…and implants. Me, I'm au natural, doncha love it? (*poses*) But seriously, I'm perfect, too. Ya gotta own it. Am I right?

BUBBA
My voice gives the audience chills.

SHECKY
So does mine.

MOM
Singing has always come naturally to Shirley. (*sings an arpeggio*)

SHECKY
Dancing is my forte (*dances…badly*)

BUBBA
Really, don't be jealous of me. I'm generous to the lesser folk, if they'd just watch and learn.

MOM
You can't teach Shirley anything. She was born perfect.

BUBBA
I happen to have an agent that my girlfriend got me.

MOM
Shirley has an agent, too.

SHECKY
I'm my own stage mother. (*to LANCE)* How do you get a part?

BUBBA
Talent and preparation.

SHECKY
Preparation H? For the H of it?

BUBBA
(*steps back as though preparing…*) "What light in yon window breaks? It is the East and Juliet is the sun."

SHECKY
(*to girl*) And what do YOU do to get the part?

MOM
Besides talent and preparation? Hairspray and lip gloss. Show them, Shirley.

SHIRLEY
(*Bad over the top read*) "If we shadows have offended, think but this and all is mended, that you have but slumber'd here, while these visions did appear. And this weak and idle theme, no more yielding but a dream." (*Opens purse, applies lip gloss*)

BUBBA
(*to SHECKY*) What do you do to get a part?

SHECKY
(*all action happens very quickly: falls on floor, "walks" in circle on side, stands up, speaks bombastically*) "All the world's a stage…." (sings) "The sun'll come out tomorrow." (*burps*) I'll do anything to get the part.

MOM, BUBBA & SHIRLEY
Does that work?

SHECKY
I booked three jobs last week, without an agent. What have you booked lately?

BUBBA
I need to call my agent.

MOM
We need a new color lip gloss.

SHECKY
Don't hate them cuz they're perfect.

Blackout

SCENE 3, YOU'RE ENOUGH

Full lights

DIRECTOR #2

Casually walks across stage, stops, addresses audience. I've always worked one way. That is, YOU'RE ENOUGH. What does that mean? Come on, think about it. You're your own gift. Take your strengths, your weaknesses, and blend them. What do you get? A total you.

> *WALLY enters,
> watches from side.*

Sure, you have to practice your craft. If it was easy, everyone would do this. Work at it. Learn and study and practice. Then you're enough for whatever comes along. Now, go out and get cast. I'll see you at the Tony's.

> *Music intro*

SCENE 3, WALTZING IN 4/4 TIME

          (WALLY)
WALTZING IN 4/4 TIME
TO ME THERE'S NO RHYTHM OR RHYME.
1-2-3, 1-2-3, 1-2-3-4.
ADDS UP TO TEN,
NOT ONE NUMBER MORE.
CAN'T DANCE A LICK.
PLEASE SHOW ME THE TRICK.
WALTZING IN 4/4 TIME.

TRYING MY BEST TO FIT IN.
BUT SEEMS THERE'S NO WAY TO WIN.
1-2-3, 1-2-3, 1-2-3-4.
MESSED UP AGAIN.
OH DANG! WHAT A CHORE.
IS THIS A QUIZ?
I'M NOT SOME MATH WHIZ.
WALTZING IN 4/4 TIME.

MOVING MY FEET TO A STRONG 4/4 BEAT.
THINK I CAN DO IT, NOW.
STEPPING IN TIME, MAYBE REACHING MY PRIME.
WATCH ME DANCING, WOW!

JUST WATCH MY SMOKE! I AM NOT GONNA CHOKE.
I'LL GLIDE JUST LIKE ASTAIRE.
UP WALLS AND DOWN, YES AND ALL AROUND THE TOWN,
MOVING WITHOUT A CARE.

RHYTHM IS STUCK IN MY MIND,
I THOUGHT I HAD LEFT THAT BEHIND.
1-2-3, 1-2-3, 1-2-3-4.
I TOLD YOU MY PROBLEMS
TWO TIMES BEFORE.
CAN'T GET IT DONE,
JUST NOT ANY FUN.
WALTZING IN 4/4 TIME.

WALTZING IN 4/4 TIME.
I'D RATHER SUCK ON A LIME.
1-2-3, 1-2-3, 1-2-3-4.
THAT'S IT! I'M HEADING
RIGHT OUT THE DOOR.
SHOES HURT MY FEET,
NOT GONNA REPEAT,
WALTZING IN 4/4 TIME.

NO MORE STAGE FRIGHT! DID YOU SEE? I GOT IT RIGHT?
FINALLY NAILED THAT BEAT.
FEET FEEL SO LIGHT, WANT TO DANCE ALL THE NIGHT.
TIME NOW TO TURN UP THE HEAT.

16 BAR DANCE BREAK

JUST WATCH MY FEET, DANCE IS SO VERY SWEET.
GLAD THAT I TOOK THAT DARE!
SUCCESS LIKE THIS, I DON'T WANNA MISS.
GREATNESS, I'LL JUST HAVE TO BEAR.
YES, GREATNESS I'LL JUST HAVE TO BEAR.

Full lights still up

SCENE 5, THEATER GAMES #2

Full lights still up

LANCE

Spotlight, please. (*Waits, nothing happens.*) More theater games, doncha just love it? Find a partner. This promotes self-assurance, looking at someone, and...uhh...ahh looking at someone. One of you is a hooty owl. The other is a rotten peach. Find common ground through you looking at someone.

Here's another great game. This one, you'll do alone. Think about food, namely tacos. Now, I want you to feel the tacos. Feeeellll the tacos. You can substitute burritos, but try to feeeellll the tacos... This teaches you to…ahhhh, well...feel the tacos. I don't know how I can make it any clearer. Feeeeellllll the tacos!

Spotlight comes on after LANCE exits, VO gives an evil laugh.

SCENE 6, DUELING DIRECTORS

Full lights

POINDEXTER
I heard they precast the show.

BERTHA
Oh, you mean Shecky? Yeah, he's sort of the flavor of the month. Or the year. At least the director doesn't cast his own kid all the time.

SHIRLEY
That's not fair! Besides, my Mom isn't a director, not really. She's just . . . super interested, wants me to succeed, and –

POINDEXTER
Hey, no blame. So, did they promise you the part, too? Nobody would turn down a promised role!

SHIRLEY
I wish. Nope, I'm not on the flavor-of-the-month club--yet. Mom's still working on that.

BERTHA
If they precast one part, what's to say they haven't promised a bunch of roles? Makes you wonder why we even try. Some really good actors I know decided not to come out.

SHIRLEY
Mom hates pre-casting. Unless it's her, of course. Some theaters post in advance what roles are available, or not.

BERTHA
I'd still hate it. But at least you'd know.

POINDEXTER
Oh well. There's always chess club. *(starts to leave)*

SHECKY
(enters with a swagger) Hey, where you going? The auditions haven't even started.

DIRECTOR #1 (OFFSTAGE)
One by one, hit your mark and slate. We're watching movement, people, this is a dance show! Then read your prepared line and sing the first phrase.

BERTHA
(pirouettes to the mark) My name is Bertha Getz. *(settles herself)* I'm not going to see you for a whole summer! *(sings)* But it's all make believe, artful blocking to deceive, it's an act, I'm so relieved…

DIRECTOR #1 (OFFSTAGE)
Next!

SHECKY
(clowns to the mark) My name is Shecky Liebowitz. *(same lines/song, a GOOD read)* I'm not going to see you for a whole summer! *(sings)* But it's all make believe, artful blocking to deceive, it's an act, I'm so relieved… *(wiggles his butt)*

DIRECTOR #1 (OFFSTAGE)
Next!

SHIRLEY
(modern dance to the mark) My name is Shirley Ann Temple.

MOM (OFFSTAGE)
TemPLER!

SHIRLEY
(same lines/song, POOR read) I'm not going to see you for a whole summer! *(sings)* But it's all make believe, artful blocking to deceive, it's an act, I'm so relieved…

> *Three DIRECTORS and MOM enter as SHIRLEY leaves.*

VOCAL COACH
(sings the phrase correctly) Thank you, dear, you can go.

DIRECTOR #1
I think it's obvious who gets the part. Shecky Liebowitz! That guy has got the goods.

MOM
Are you kidding me?

CHOREOGRAPHER
It IS a dance show. Bertha nailed it, she's so graceful.

MOM
But Bertha's pipes can't compare to Shirley's. Such a voice!

DIRECTOR #1
I still love Shecky! And I sort of already promised him the role.

(others stare daggers at him)

There's a lot riding on this production, to deliver the kind of performance audiences have come to expect. What if nobody good auditions? I've already taught the rest of them everything I know, and they still suck! At least Shecky delivers. He can act the song.

CHOREOGRAPHER
He can't act the dance. I've already got the numbers choreographed. And Bertha has a…pleasant voice. Granted, her cold reads stinks, but that'll improve with rehearsal.

MOM
She sings better than Shecky, I'll give you that. My Shirley nailed the dance. And the song. What ever happened to triple threats?

DIRECTOR #1
I'll triple threat you if we don't cast Shecky. I can work with him. You can't just precast your own kid every time. *(Sees someone sidle onto stage)* Can I help you? We're confabbing here.

POINDEXTER
Am I too late? Can I still audition?

DIRECTOR #1
(a beat) No.

STARZ, the MUSICAL

                    CHOREO & V-COACH (*together*)
Yes.

                         DIRECTOR #1
I can't work like this! (*flounces off to the side*)

                            MOM
We're…I mean THEY are looking for strong singers…

                       CHOREOGRAPHER
…and dancers. I can teach, if you can move with grace and confidence.

                         DIRECTOR #1
And actors with comic timing. And pathos, don't forget the pathos!

                       CHOREOGRAPHER
Show us what you've got. Slate, then a little movement, please. Then give us your best read and sing the first phrase.

                          POINDEXTER
(*very shy, waves*) My name is Sydney Poindexter. (*suddenly comes alive, with a spontaneous dance. Gives GREAT read*). I'm not going to see you for a whole summer! (*sings*) But it's all make believe, artful blocking to deceive, it's an act, I'm so relieved, the kissing isn't real.

                           SILENCE.

                          POINDEXTER
Was that okay?

                          DIRECTORS
(*nod, point for her to leave*)

                CHOREOGRAPHER & VOCAL COACH (together)
(*to DIRECTOR #1*) And that's what I call a triple threat.

                         DIRECTOR #1
You want a triple threat? I'll give you a triple threat. Mayo in your toe-shoes, I'll spit in your pitch pipe, and and and…I'll even, I'll put an anvil in your purse.

                            MOM
What does that mean?

DIRECTOR #1
I don't know. But it's gonna happen, mark my words. Because I said so. I'm the director. It's my show! And besides, Poindexter doesn't fit the suit! I've already rented the costumes.

Full lights continue, intro song.

SCENE 7, DUELING DIRECTORS (SONG)

(VOCAL COACH)

HE CAN'T SING.
CAN'T MATCH TONE.
RUSTY HINGE THAT
MAKES YOU CRINGE.
NO, HE CAN'T
SING. BUT…

(MOM)

NOT HER THING.
MOANS AND GROANS.
MUSIC SCARES BUT
ACTOR DARES.
BUT NOT HER
THING. BUT…

(CHOREO)

HE CAN'T SWING,
LEAVE ALONE.
RHYTHMIC DANCING,
HE'S NOT CHANCING
HE CAN'T
SWING. BUT…

(DIRECTOR #1)

ACTING SCENES,
LINES ARE BLOWN.
HOGGING SPOTLIGHTS
GETTING STAGE FRIGHT,
ACTING SCENES. BUT…

STARZ, the MUSICAL

Sung in a "round." VOCAL COACH begins alone and sings total 3 times, each part comes in following previous part.

(VOCAL COACH)	(MOM)	(CHOREO)	(DIRECTOR)
HE CAN'T SING. CAN'T MATCH TONE. RUSTY HINGE THAT MAKES YOU CRINGE. NO, HE CAN'T SING. BUT…	NOT HER THING. MOANS AND GROANS. MUSIC SCARES BUT ACTOR DARES. BUT NOT HER THING. BUT…	HE CAN'T SWING, LEAVE ALONE. RHYTHM DANCING, HE'S NOT CHANCING S/HE CAN'T SWING. BUT…	ACTING SCENES, LINES ARE BLOWN. HOGGING SPOTLIGHTS GETTING STAGE FRIGHT, ACTING SCENES. BUT…

(ACTORS-unison one time, then in round with directors)
NOW WE SING/SWING
ON OUR OWN.
SONGS AND DANCING
LINE ENHANCING
NOW WE SING/SWING. OH…

NOW WE SING/SWING ON OUR OWN. SONGS AND DANCING LINE ENHANCING NOW WE SING/SWING. OH…	NOW WE SING/SWING ON OUR OWN. SONGS AND DANCING LINE ENHANCING NOW WE SING/SWING. OH..	NOW WE SING/SWING ON OUR OWN. SONGS AND DANCING LINE ENHANCING NOW WE SING/SWING. OH…	NOW THEY SING/SWING ON THEIR OWN. SONGS AND DANCING LINE ENHANCING NOW THEY SING/SWING. OH…
NOW WE SING!	NOW WE SWING!	IN OUR ZONE!	ON THEIR OWN!

Blackout

SCENE 8, KNOW IT ALL ACTOR #4

Blackout continues

LANCE
(Carries flashlight, takes place, shines light in his own face.) This comes from Nancy Smith in Taos, New Mexico. She asks, "I see actors kiss on screen. Are they really kissing, or is it camera angles that make it look like they're kissing?"

Well, Carlotta, first of all it's good to hear from our friends south of the border. Cameras are a tricky thing. As you might know, extension cords carry electricity, and if you get one wet that has a hole in it, it can sure shock you. *Tries to shut off flashlight, bangs it, still won't go off, he EXITS speaking...* That's what happens when techies let you down.

SCENE 9, STAGE CRUSH

Stage right area light

POINDEXTER
I'm really glad we got cast. Together, I mean.

BUBBA
Me too, I guess.

POINDEXTER
I've never had a romantic part before.

BUBBA
I've never had a part at all. My girlfriend talked me into this.

POINDEXTER
Will she get mad? We're supposed to kiss.

BUBBA
I don't think so. She's the actor person. She should understand about stuff like this.

POINDEXTER
What about you? I feel kind of weird, you know? Not that you're not…oh never mind. *(shy)*

BUBBA
Don't we just do what the director says? Isn't that the way it works?

POINDEXTER
If you don't want to, kiss I mean, you probably shouldn't have taken the part.

BUBBA
They fake kisses sometimes, right?

POINDEXTER
(disappointed) I guess.

BUBBA
I'm just here because my girlfriend made me. If she gets jealous it's her own fault. Stage kiss doesn't mean a thing.

POINDEXTER
(really disappointed) You're right. To really matter, it's got to be more than acting.

VO
Take it from your last line.

Music intro

BUBBA
(assumes "actor" voice) I'm not going to see you for a whole summer. *(He kisses her, she melts. He sees girlfriend offstage, and breaks)* Hey wait up, I'm nearly done here. *(hurries away, exits.)*

Introduction to song

SCENE 10, WHEN KISSES DON'T MATTER

Sings in stage R area light

(POINDEXTER)
HE TAKES MY HAND.
WE SHARE GLANCE,
UNTIL THE BAND
BEGINS THE DANCE.

NOW CHEEK TO CHEEK,
GLIDE TO THE LEFT.
HE TURNS AWAY,
I FEEL BEREFT.

BUT IT'S ALL MAKE BELIEVE,
ARTFUL BLOCKING TO DECEIVE.
IT'S AN ACT, DON'T BE NAÏVE.
THE KISSING ISN'T REAL.

AUDIENCES WILL PERCEIVE
WHAT DIRECTORS HAVE CONCEIVED,
TRUE EMOTION'S NOT ACHIEVED
FROM KISSES THAT YOU STEAL.

Stage R light fades, stage L area light comes up, BUBBA enters and sings.

(BUBBA)

SHE TAKES MY HAND.
WE SHARE GLANCE,
THAT IS THE CUE
TO BEGIN ROMANCE.

OUR LIPS DRAW NEAR...
I HOLD MY BREATH.
SHE LOOKED AWAY,
AND THEN SHE LEFT.
IT'S A LITTLE DEATH.

BUT IT'S ALL MAKE BELIEVE,
ARTFUL BLOCKING TO DECEIVE.
IT'S AN ACT, I'M SO RELIEVED
THE KISSING ISN'T REAL.

AUDIENCES WILL PERCEIVE
WHAT DIRECTORS HAVE CONCEIVED.
TRUE EMOTIONS NOT RECEIVED
FROM KISSES THAT YOU STEAL.

POINDEXTER and BUBBA meet center stage, all lights up, they dance (32 measures waltz)

(POINDEXTER)	(BUBBA)
BUT IT'S ALL MAKE BELIEVE,	
	ARTFUL BLOCKING TO DECEIVE,
IT'S AN ACT.	
	WE'RE SO RELIEVED
THE KISSING ISN'T REAL.	THE KISSING ISN'T REAL.
AUDIENCES WILL PERCEIVE WHAT DIRECTORS HAVE CONCEIVED TRUE EMOTION'S NOT ACHIEVED FROM KISSES THAT YOU STEAL.	AUDIENCES WILL PERCEIVE WHAT DIRECTORS HAVE CONCEIVED TRUE EMOTION'S NOT ACHIEVED FROM KISSES THAT YOU STEAL.
WHEN KISSES DON'T MATTER	
	IGNORE ANY CHATTER
UNLESS IF YOU'D RATHER KISS! FOR REAL… AND SEE HOW YOU FEEL.	UNLESS YOU'D RATHER KISS! FOR REAL… AND SEE HOW YOU FEEL.

They start to slowly kiss—before lips meet they freeze and BLACKOUT.

SCENE 11, KNOW IT ALL ACTOR #5

LANCE walks to mark in blackout, lights candle with BIC lighter, holds flame up to read card.

LANCE
(*spooky voice*) Wooooooo, I love this one from Jimmy John Jones in prison. He writes, "I enjoy plays and movies with animals. How much training goes into making them animals do what they're supposed to do?"

Say, Ronnie Don, this is a good question. I had a dog once. Had a cat, too. And, parrots live a couple of hundred years. Thanks for the question.
(*Yelps when wax burns fingers, and blows candle out.*)

SCENE 12, CRY BABY, CRY

> *Actors each in his/her own area light SR, C and SL, speaking to audience but "answering" each other.*

SHIRLEY
(with box of Kleenex) My dog died today at 12:37. I have a matinee at 2:00. How do I not cry? I sing all the happy songs in the show.

BERTHA
I have an audition today at 2:00, and this director really wants me to get into the emotion of the character. I'm screwed.

WALLY
I can cry anytime I want. It impresses the directors, the audience, and heck, even me sometimes. Crying on cue is easy.

BERTHA
How do you cry on cue? I don't even cry at sad movies.

WALLY
Crying on cue is easy…and it's not. I have to re-live something painful. Like disappointing Dad.

SHIRLEY
I know the show must go on. There's no understudy. The whole cast depends on me. But how can I get through it? A box of Kleenex in the wings is too simple. I don't know if I can do this.

BERTHA
I can do drama. I can scream and moan, and get angry. I'm reading for a great part, where my best friend just died. I know they'll expect me to cry. Maybe if I put an onion in my pocket or something.

SHIRLEY
My mom says I can use this someday, maybe in a drama. But I don't want to think about that. I miss my dog. And my drama teacher told us, "Remember, you're the character. The character is not you." I just gotta remember that.

WALLY
But every time I pull up that hurt, that sorrow, it takes something out of me. And I've started to ask myself, do I really want to go there, to that painful place, all over again? For the show—for the character. Yeah, I guess I do.

                    BERTHA
(with onion) Yeah, an onion, this will work.

                    DIR. #2
Lose the damn onion, kid. You smell like pickled hair.

                    BERTHA
(look at onion, and toss it)

                    SHIRLEY
Okay, gotta put on my game face and sparkle. (*takes on happy expression, and deflates*) I feel like a fake. But I guess that's what an actor does.

                    WALLY
Here I go. *(takes a moment, looks down, and back up and tears flow)*

                    DIR. #2
Nice tears, but you're trying too hard. Salt and pepper, kid, like seasoning, too much spoils the scene. And if you cry, the audience won't need to.

                    BERTHA
I have a best friend. He/she drove me here. I'd feel like crap if he/she died.

                    SHIRLEY
My dog loved to hear me sing. She'd howl along. Okay, Fluffy…today the show's just for you.

                              Slow blackout

SCENE 13, RESPECT

                              Enters with follow spot to center stage.

                    STAGE MANAGER
I hate the spotlight, can you dial it down, please? Just give me some work lights. (*Spotlight goes out, goes to blues.*) I'm the stage manager. Also known as the Boss, Ms/Mr Big, The authority, the final say, Almighty Me. This is how I see myself. To the actors and crew, I'm the jerk, the creep, the know-it-all, pushy son of a …peach.

   I never cared about stepping into the spotlight, but it's not a power trip or shyness that makes me love my behind-the-scenes job. It's more than wearing headphones and holding a clipboard—it's holding everyone to the highest possible standard. I'm a conductor—just like the one waving a baton to keep the beat going—only I make sure the actors, sets, lights and sound come together in the right harmony. If I do my job right, I'm totally invisible to the audience. But not to my crew.

I'm the first one to show up, and the last one to leave. If I'm a hardcase, it's cuz I want the show to be great. And you have to train them right, to jump when they need to. Like this…

PLACES! *(Groups of actors run across stage, total chaos, and stop in pre-assigned spots in poses.)* Am I good or what? *(Costumer sneaks in from the other side to takes place…sewing last bits on a costume)*.

It's all about respect. We all want the same thing, and somebody's got to drive the train. I have to earn their respect, though, and it goes both ways. They respect me, but by golly, I respect them back.

Heck, there's no way I could ever sing and dance like *(POINT TO CHARACTER who dances/sings off stage)*, or sew costumes like NAME *(the late comer hands costume to actor, and they both leave)*, or slap paint and slam a hammer with such artistry *(crew leaves)*, shine a light or boost a mic, or create props and makeup effects the audience loves. Yeah, I love my job. And the techies, they're more invisible heroes. But we're all in this together, right?

SCENE 14, WHEN TECHIES LET YOU DOWN

Still in blues, enough to fully light stage

(ACTORS)
WHEN MY MIC GOES DEAD,
AND MY LINES GO UNSAID,
IT'S EVERYTHING I DREAD,
WHEN TECHIES LET YOU DOWN…

WE RELY ON EXPERTISE.	WE NEED YOUR FINESSE
NO EXCUSE, NO TIME TO FIGHT.	YOUR BEST, CUZ
PLEASE HAVE OUR BACK,	THERE'S NO BLAME
WE WON'T ATTACK,	WE'RE ALL THE SAME
LET'S DO THIS MAKE IT RIGHT.	LET'S DO THIS MAKE IT RIGHT.

WHEN MY COSTUME
RIPS A SEAM,
AND THE PROP PHONE
DOESN'T RING,
THE SHOW WON'T MEAN
A THING
IF TECHIES LET YOU
DOWN

WE RELY ON EXPERTISE
NO EXCUSE, NO TIME TO FIGHT
PLEASE HAVE OUR BACK,
WE WON'T ATTACK,
LET'S DO THIS, MAKE IT RIGHT.

WE NEED YOUR FINESSE
YOUR BEST, CUZ
THERE'S NO BLAME
WE'RE ALL THE SAME
LET'S DO THIS, MAKE IT RIGHT.

(TECHIE RAP-STAGE MANAGER, SHIRLEY, LANCE & TRIO)

WHY AM I HERE, TO SUPPORT THE ACTOR?
WE'RE NOT JUST THAT, IT JUST DON'T FACTOR.
GOT HAMMERS, GOT WIGS, GOT MAKE-UP, TOO.
GOT LIGHT BULBS, GOT COSTUMES, TO NAME A FEW.

WE'RE BIG STRONG GUYS, AND CREATIVE GIRLS.
WE CAN DECK YOU OUT ARMY, OR GO FLUFFY CURLS.
GOT NAIL GUNS, GOT DRILL GUNS, GOT BIG OL' CLAMPS.
GOT MICS FOR SOUND, AND GREAT BIG AMPS.

I'M TECH, YA KNOW, GOT BRAGGIN' RIGHTS.
WE MAKE ACTORS LOOK GOOD IN DARKEST NIGHTS.
GOT MAKE-UP SPONGES, LOTS OF POWDER, TOO.
GOT SCARY WIGS, OH YEAH, JUST TRY A FEW.

WE'RE BIG STRONG GUYS, AND CREATIVE GIRLS.
WE CAN DECK YOU OUT ARMY, OR GO FLUFFY CURLS.
GOT NAIL GUNS, GOT DRILL GUNS, GOT BIG OL' CLAMPS.
GOT MICS FOR SOUND, AND GREAT BIG AMPS.

WE'RE TECH! LET'S HEAR IT FOR ALL OF US.
MESS WITH US ONLY IF YOU WANT A FUSS.
GOT SCISSORS, GAFFERS TAPE, AND EVEN ELMER'S GLUE.
(SISSY VOICE) I COULD HURT YOU, THERE, ACTOR. YEP, IT'S TRUE.

WE'RE BIG, WE'RE STRONG AND THE BRIGHTEST OF BRIGHT
RUNNING TECH GIVES US LOTS OF BRAGGIN' RIGHTS.
MESS WITH US AND YOU WILL GET A FUSS,
WE'RE TECH, LET'S HEAR IT FOR ALL OF US.

lights up, down, spots, etc.

(TECHIES/SUNG)
TIME TO CHECK, CHECK, CHECK,
OUT THE SOUND, SOUND, SOUND,
CLEAR THE DECK, DECK, DECK,
LOOK AROUND, 'ROUND, 'ROUND

SET THE LIGHTS, LIGHTS, LIGHTS,
FIX YOUR TIGHTS, TIGHTS, TIGHTS,
SEE WHAT'S FOUND, FOUND, FOUND.
WE NEVER LET YOU DOWN.

(ACTORS)	(TECHIES)
WHEN THE PAINT AIN'T DRY,	TIME TO CHECK, CHECK, CHECK
AND SET PIECES JUST WON'T FLY,	OUT THE SOUND, SOUND, SOUND,
THE SPOTLIGHT SHINES TOO HIGH,	CLEAR THE DECK, DECK, DECK,
WHEN TECHIES LET YOU DOWN.	LOOK AROUND, 'ROUND, 'ROUND
WE RELY ON EXPERTISE	SET THE LIGHTS, LIGHTS, LIGHTS,
NO EXCUSE, NO TIME TO FIGHT	FIX YOUR TIGHTS, TIGHTS, TIGHTS,
PLEASE HAVE OUR BACK,	SEE WHAT'S FOUND, FOUND FOUND.
WE WON'T ATTACK,	WE NEVER LET
LET'S DO THIS, MAKE IT RIGHT.	YOU DOWN.

WHEN THE SET FALLS TO THE FLOOR	TIME TO CHECK, CHECK, CHECK,
AND THE KNOB'S OFF THE DOOR	OUT THE SOUND, SOUND, SOUND,
FAKE NOSES JUST WON'T SNORE,	CLEAR THE DECK, DECK, DECK,
WHEN TECHIES LET YOU DOWN.	LOOK AROUND, 'ROUND, 'ROUND
WE RELY ON EXPERTISE	SET THE LIGHTS, LIGHTS, LIGHTS,
NO EXCUSE, NO TIME TO FIGHT	FIX YOUR TIGHTS, TIGHTS, TIGHTS,
PLEASE HAVE OUR BACK,	SEE WHAT'S FOUND,
WE WON'T ATTACK, LET'S DO THIS, MAKE IT RIGHT.	FOUND, FOUND. WE NEVER LET YOU DOWN.

Full lights

WHEN THE SET FALLS TO THE FLOOR	
	AND THE KNOB FALLS OFF THE DOOR.
FAKE NOSES JUST WON'T SNORE WHEN TECHIES LET YOU DOWN.	WHEN TECHIES LET YOU DOWN.
WE RELY ON EXPERTISE	SET THE LIGHTS, LIGHTS, LIGHTS,
NO EXCUSE, NO TIME TO FIGHT	FIX YOUR TIGHTS, TIGHTS, TIGHTS,
PLEASE HAVE OUR BACK, WE WON'T ATTACK,	SEE WHAT'S FOUND, FOUND, FOUND. WE NEVER LET YOU DOWN.
YOU NEVER LET US WE'LL NEVER LET YOU NEVER LET US DOWN.	NEVER LET YOU DOWN. NEVER LET US DOWN.

Blackout

SCENE 15, FATHER & SON 2

WALLY and DAD in two separate area lights, opposite sides of stage.

WALLY
I know how this sounds. I'm embarrassed to … wait, I'm not embarrassed at all. I was enough. And I was great. I was everything I knew I could be.

DAD
I hate to admit it…wait, I don't hate to admit it. That kid was great. He sang, he danced, he was…(*starting to tear up*) well, he was . . .

WALLY
I hope Dad wasn't disappointed. This was ME, not what he wanted me to be. But all me.

DAD
I still don't get it. I mean, there was talking, I get that. But right in the middle of a good or bad situation, they sing and dance.

WALLY
I never knew I could sing or dance. Really! But I could. I learned, just like Dad learned to bowl to please his father. He's a good bowler. And I'm a real good singer. Dancer, too.

DAD
I've got to let him know how proud I am. There's got to be something. I've got it. (*scribbles a note*)

WALLY
The fact that Dad showed up means everything. I've got to do something. I've got it! (*crosses to DAD*)

CENTER area light

DAD
(*crosses to son, sheepish*) You were great. I'm so proud.

WALLY
Really? Wow, thank you, Dad. Thank you for…

DAD

Say, I've got something for you. *(pause)* It's just a, a little something that *(pauses)* I mean, you might not want it. *(fumbles with the paper)*

WALLY

I have something for you, too. *(hands program from his play)* It's signed, Dad, by everyone in the cast. And…

DAD

Here's a note from you. *(reads aloud)* "To Dad, my #1 supporter, and my friend." *(tears up)*

WALLY

Do you like it?

DAD

More than… *(wipes eyes, blows nose)*. Here. *(takes off Cabella's hat)* You take this. This is my lucky hat. And this, too. *(offers the crumpled paper)*

WALLY

(reads the note silently) Wow Dad, you wrote a poem? It's really good!

DAD

(shrugs, embarrassed but pleased)

WALLY

(wipes eyes) You wanna hear a song?

DAD

(smiles) You wanna bowl a game?

WALLY & DAD

(almost unison) Yeah, a lot…a lot! *(exit, Dad's arm around WALLY)*

Blackout

Scene 16, STARZ FINALE

Full lights

(GIRLS) | (BOYS)

(GIRLS)
THIS MAGIC
THAT WE WEAVE.

(BOYS)
IT'S NOT JUST
MAKE BELIEVE.

(GIRLS)
WE'RE ARTISTS
YOUNG AND OLD,
THAT'S HOW OUR
STORY'S TOLD,
AND YOU
COMPLETE THE TALE.

WHEN AUDIENCE
BELIEVES

(BOYS)
WE'RE ARTISTS
YOUNG AND OLD,
THAT'S HOW OUR
STORY'S TOLD,
AND YOU
COMPLETE THE TALE.

WE'RE GIVEN A
REPRIEVE.

(GIRLS)
FORGIVE THE
ALLEGORY,
RELEASED FROM
PURGATORY!
OUR EFFORTS
DIDN'T FAIL!

(BOYS)
FORGIVE THE
ALLEGORY,
RELEASED FROM
PURGATORY!
OUR EFFORTS
DIDN'T FAIL!

(ALL)
A LITTLE LEFT OF CENTER,
A LITTLE IN THE WRONG?
EV'RY MISFIT,
GETS A PERMIT,
JOIN OUR FAMILY!
YOU BELONG.

FOREVER PERFECTING
THE CRAFT WE ARE MAKING

                          THE AUDIENCE ENERGY
                          SWEETENS THE DREAM.

TOGETHER WE'RE BETTER.	TOGETHER WE'RE BETTER.
PLEASE, LEND US YOUR EAR!	PLEASE, LEND US YOUR EAR!
PERFORMANCE IS LONELY	PERFORMANCE IS LONELY
WITH NO ONE TO HEAR!	WITH NO ONE TO HEAR!

(ALL)

I'LL TRUST MY HEART, TRY ONE MORE DAY
TO GET THE PART, CAN'T STAY AWAY.
IT'S WHO I AM. DREAMS NEVER DIE,
HOWEVER LONG THE DREAMERS TRY.
HOWEVER LONG THE DREAMERS TRY.

(GIRLS)   *(BOYS)*

FOREVER PERFECTING
THE CRAFT WE ARE MAKING

                          THE TALENT WE BRING
                          THAT COMPOSES THE DREAM.

(ALL)

TOGETHER WE'RE BETTER.
BE GENEROUS, FRIEND.
NO SOLO IS SOLO
WHEN ALL OF US WIN!

IT'S NOT ABOUT THE BEING,
BUT RATHER ALL THE REACHING
TO THE STARZ! TO THE STARZ!

IT'S NOT ABOUT ARRIVING,
BUT EVERYONE WHO'S STRIVING
FOR THE STARZ! FOR THE STARZ!

FOR THE STARZ!

CURTAIN

MUSICAL NUMBERS

ACT 1

1: *Misfit* (Company)..77

2: *My Way, Or The Highway* (Dirs, Company)............................80

3: *Sparkle* (Mom, Shirley)..85

4A: *Boogie Woogie Laffs* (Shecky)..92

4B: *Boogie Woogie Laffs* (Shecky)..95

5: *In It For The Babes* (Chance, Trio)..98

6: *Starz* (Bertha, Wally, Mom, Shirley).....................................106

7: *Make Me Proud* (Dad)..109

8: *Fit The Suit* (Company)..111

Act 2

9: *Dreams Never Die* (Dir.2)..119

10: *Waltzing In 4/4 Time* (Wally)...121

11: *Dueling Directors* (Dirs, Company)...................................123

12: *When Kisses Don't Matter* (Poindexter, Bubba)................129

13: *When Techies Let You Down* (Company)..........................134

14: *Starz Finale* (Company)...144

1. Misfit

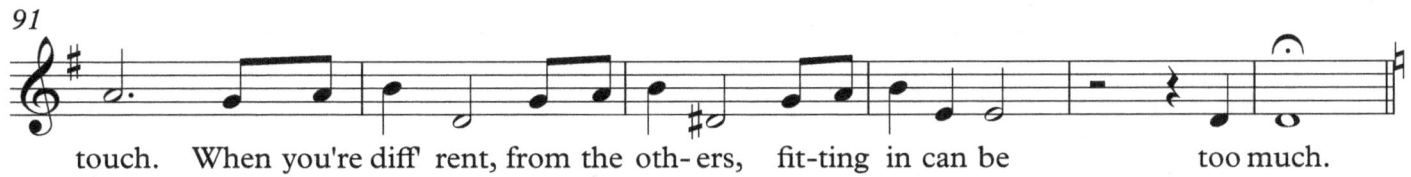

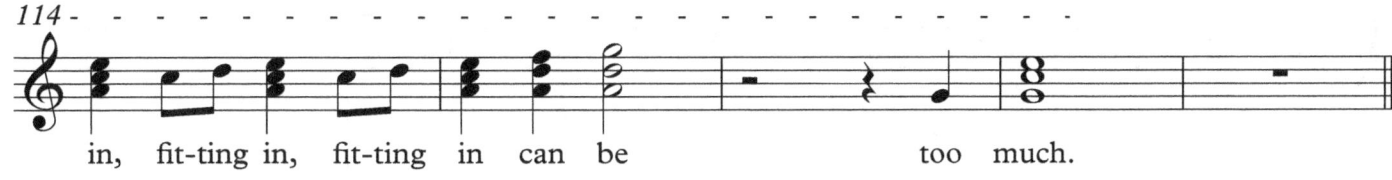

2. My Way Or The Highway

Amy Shojai/Frank Steele

3. Sparkle

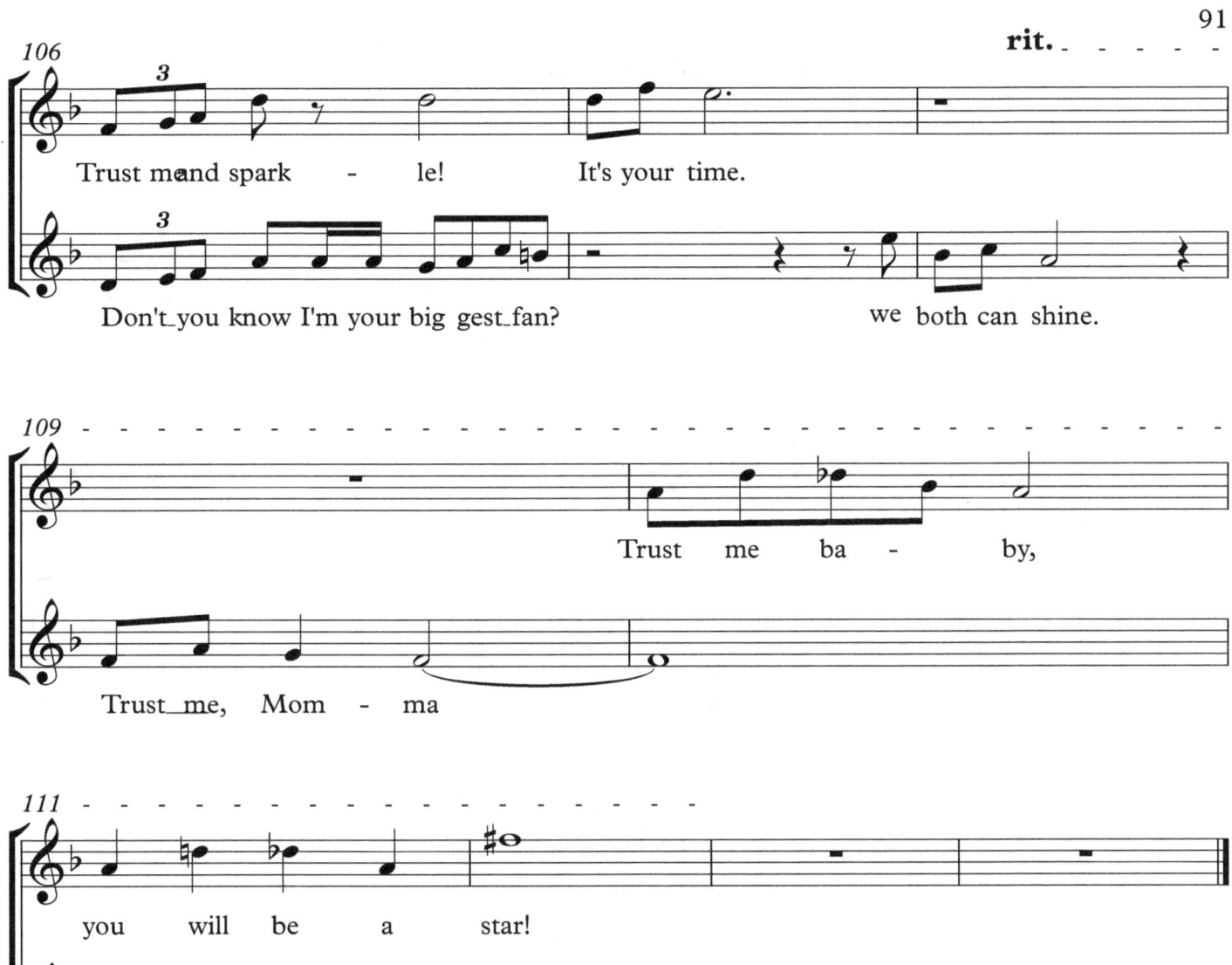

4. Boogie Woogie Laffs

Frank Steele/Amy Shojai
♩ = 150

Frank Steele.Amy Shojai

Well, I'm real-ly stead-y Fred-dy, got a joke at the read-y, gon-na get a big laugh or smile. Five'll get ya fif-ty, gon-na think I'm kind-a nif-ty, gon-na make ya laugh quite a while. Man, it's what I do, I do the fun-ny through and through, I'm shar-ing all my wit with you. You're gon-na love it! Since I'm tru-ly fun-ny Fred, I'll wear a box-er or a ted-dy, an-y thing to get a grin. My style is kind-a hot, ya might like it, may-be not. Gon-na hit the com-mic spin. Man, it's what I do, I do the fun-ny through and through. I'm gon-na be a hit with you. You're gon-na love it!

Copyright © 2017

I feed my cow sawdust instead of hay. The milk tastes okay, but I'm pretty tired of drinking the splinters. (RIMSHOT)

A preacher tells his flock, "Take all the whisky bottles in your house and thrown them in the river. Take all the whisky bottles on your street, and throw them in the river. Take all the whisky bottles in the town and throw themin the river. Now, let us all sing, "Shall We Gather At the River." (RIMSHOT)

Hey there, pretty Betty, since you know me, clever Freddy, does my comedy work for

you? Got a million jokes, I'll even try 'em on your folks. Some are kind-a old, some new.

Man, it's what I do. I do the funny through and through. I'll do a bit for

you. You're gonna love it! Since I'm dang funny Freddy and my

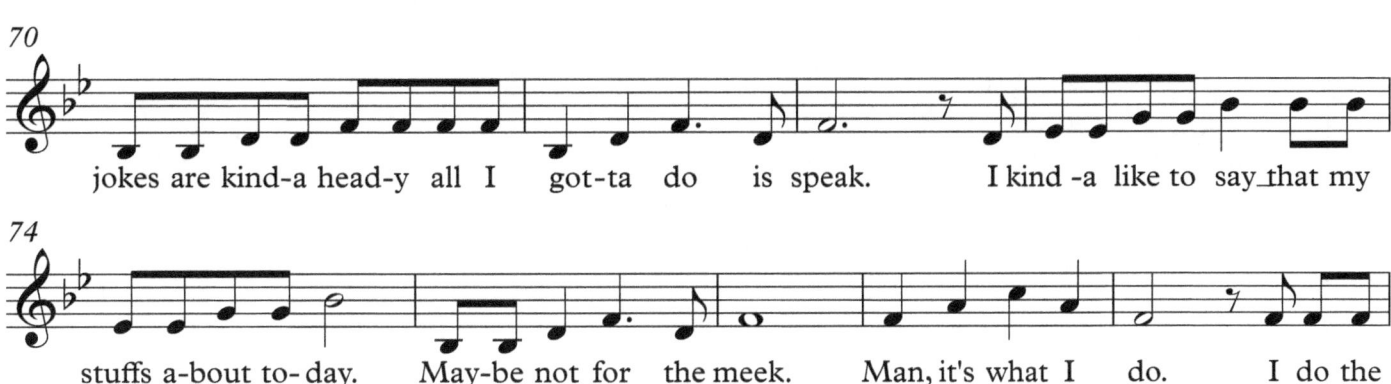

jokes are kind-a heady all I gotta do is speak. I kind-a like to say that my stuffs about today. Maybe not for the meek. Man, it's what I do. I do the

fun-ny through and through. I'm on fire, and lit for you. You're gon-na love it!

A man walks into a shoe store and asks, "Do you have alligator shoes? The clerk says, "Well, bring your alligator in and we'll try to fit him." (RIMSHOT)

A ventriloquist and his dummy walk into a bar. Bar tender says, "What'll you have?" Ventriloquist says, "I'll have a double ginger ale. But I can't speak for the other guy." (RIMSHOT)

Man, it's what I do. I do the fun - ny through and through. I'll tell a joke and sit with you. You're gon-na love it!

4. Boogie Woogie Laffs

Frank Steele/Amy Shojai
♩ = 150

Frank Steele.Amy Shojai

Well, I'm real-ly stead-y Fred-dy, got a joke at the read-y, gon-na get a big laugh or smile. Five'll get ya fif-ty, gon-na think I'm kind-a nif-ty, gon-na make ya laugh quite a while. Man, it's what I do, I do the fun-ny through and through, I'm shar-ing all my wit with you. You're gon-na love it! Since I'm tru-ly fun-ny Fred, I'll wear a box-er or a ted-dy, an-y thing to get a grin. My style is kind-a hot, ya might like it, may-be not. Gon-na hit the com-mic spin. Man, it's what I do, I do the fun-ny through and through. I'm gon-na be a hit with

Copyright © 2017

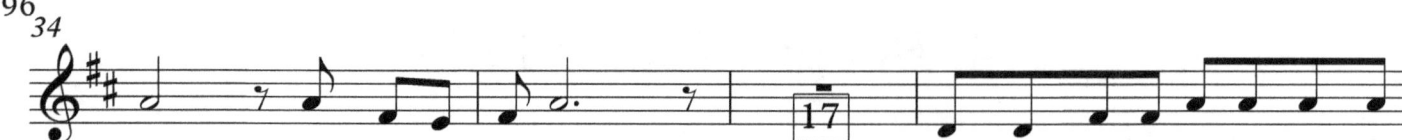

I feed my cow sawdust instead of hay. The milk tastes okay, but I'm pretty tired of drinking the splinters. (RIMSHOT)

A preacher tells his flock, "Take all the whisky bottles in your house and thrown them in the river. Take all the whisky bottles on your street, and throw them in the river. Take all the whisky bottles in the town and throw them in the river. Now, let us all sing, "Shall We Gather At the River." (RIMSHOT)

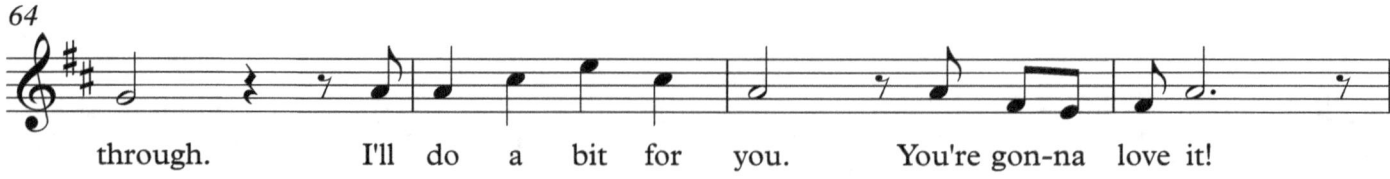

A man walks into a shoe store and asks, "Do you have alligator shoes? The clerk says, "Well, bring your alligator in and we'll try to fit him." (RIMSHOT)

A ventriloquist and his dummy walk into a bar. Bar tender says, "What'll you have?" Ventriloquist says, "I'll have a double ginger ale. But I can't speak for the other guy."
(RIMSHOT)

5. I'm In It For The Babes

Frank Steele/Amy Shojai

Frank Steele/Amy Shojai

Yes, he's in it. He's in it for the babes, cuz the babes kind a like what I do.

in it, watch him work. Heck, my goodness, it's true.
Yes, I'm in it! I can

act, when I do, it brings a tear. It can bring a smile or a little fear.

Shake-spear, Ib-sen, bring them on. Might scare me just a little but not for long! I'm

You're in it, for the babes, and we're go-ing cra-zy ov-er you.
Yes, I'm in it! I'm in it
Yes, you're in it! You can
All I can say, it's what I was meant to do!
out-sing Si-na-tra, you can out-dance Fred. Your act-ing puts O-liv-i-e

6. Starz

Amy Shojai/Frank Steele
♩ = 100

Amy Shojai/Frank Steele

BERTHA: It's on-ly make be-lieve. It's on-ly make be-lieve. The grown-ups all per ceive, it's sim-ple lies we weave, we're play-ing with the facts. It's on-ly make be-lieve. They think it's make be-lieve. A child-ren's game that's fake. There's so much more at stake. For us, it's not an act.

MOM: A lit-tle left of cen-ter, a lit-tle out of touch. When you're diff'rent, from the oth-ers, fit-ting in can be too much.

WALLY: They say, "Don't be nai-ve, It's on-ly make be-lieve." Per-form-ers all con ceive, our gifts are what we leave, and we will have your back.

Copyright © 2017

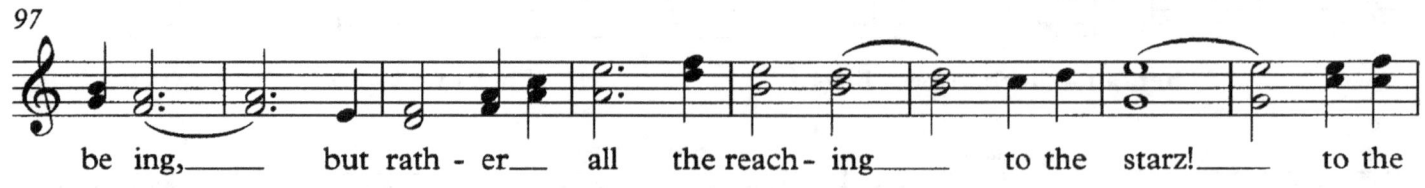

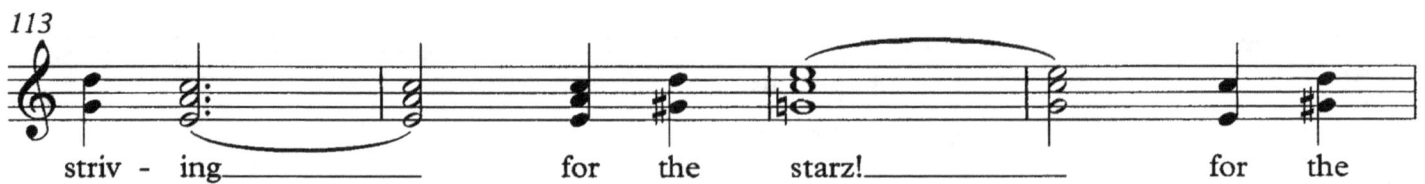

7. Make Me Proud

Frank Steele/Amy Shojai
♩ = 130

Amy Shojai/Frank Steele

Make me proud, by gol-ly, make me proud. On the field of play, yell it good and loud. Gon-na spike that ball, sum-mer spring or fall! Make me

♩ = 60

proud, by gol-ly, al-ways make me proud.

(spoken) Do I mean that? Sure, I do. I think I do. I want to . . . but my son (softly), my son . . .

♩ = 55

Make me to know you, my boy. Have__ me know you, my boy. Let's for-get all the strife, you're the whole of my life. How should I know you, my boy? Can__ I know you, my boy? Do__ I know you, my boy? These feel-ings cut like a knife, you're the whole of my life. How should I know you, my

Copyright © 2017

8. Fit The Suit

9. Dreams Never Die

Amy Shojai/Frank Steele   Amy Shojai/Frank Steele

I've got to try just one more day. Can't say good-bye, won't go a-way. It's who I

am, it's what I do. Please love me back, cuz I love you. I just can't lie, can on-ly

say how hard I try, my dues I pay. It's who I am, it's what I do. Please love me

back, cuz I love you. Your pro-mise is bro-ken when

hopes go un - spo - ken, a tra - ge - dy sea-soned with what-ifs and tears. Com -

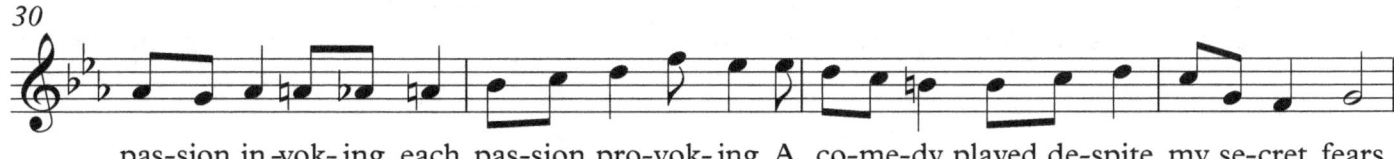
pas-sion in-vok-ing, each pas-sion pro-vok-ing. A co-me-dy played de-spite my se-cret fears.

Can't change my heart, what e'er I lack, I play my part! Please love me back. It's what I

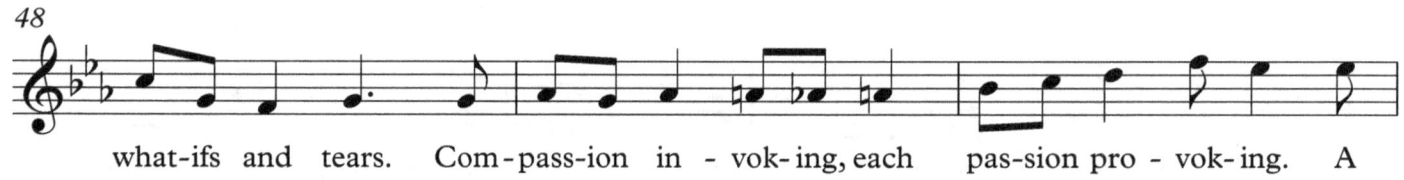

11. DUELING DIRECTORS

12. When Kisses Don't Matter

lieved. The kissing isn't real. Audiences

will perceive what directors have conceived.

True emotion's not received from kisses that you steal.

But it's all make believe,

artful blocking to deceive.

It's an act. The kissing isn't real.

We're so relieved The kissing isn't real.

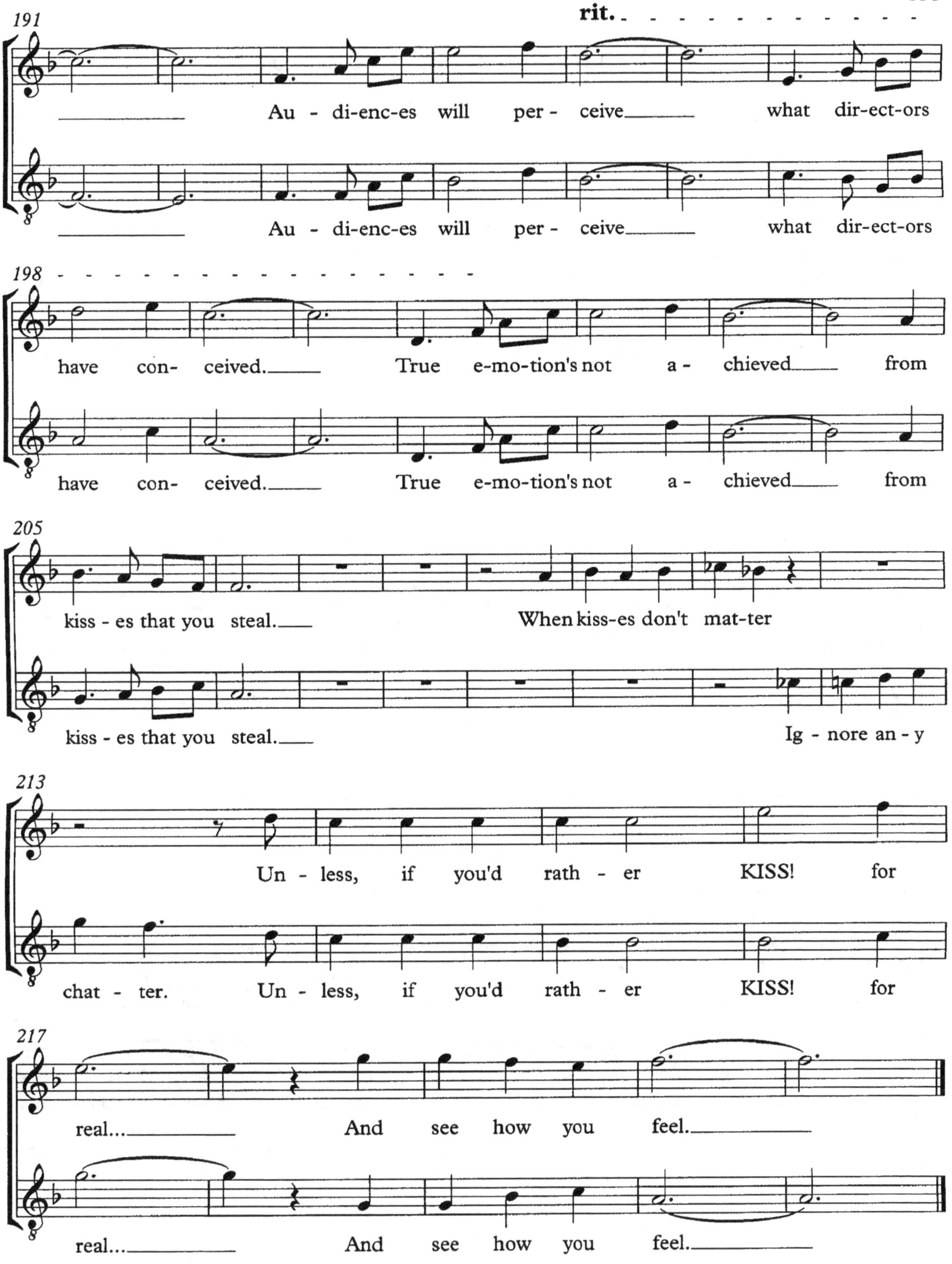
191
rit.
Au - di-enc-es will per - ceive what dir-ect-ors
Au - di-enc-es will per - ceive what dir-ect-ors
198
have con- ceived. True e-mo-tion's not a - chieved from
have con- ceived. True e-mo-tion's not a - chieved from
205
kiss - es that you steal. When kiss-es don't mat-ter
kiss - es that you steal. Ig - nore an - y
213
Un - less, if you'd rath - er KISS! for
chat - ter. Un - less, if you'd rath - er KISS! for
217
real... And see how you feel.
real... And see how you feel.

13. When Techies Let You Down & Techie Rap

Amy Shojai/Frank Steele

Amy Shojai/Frank Steele

Copyright © 2017

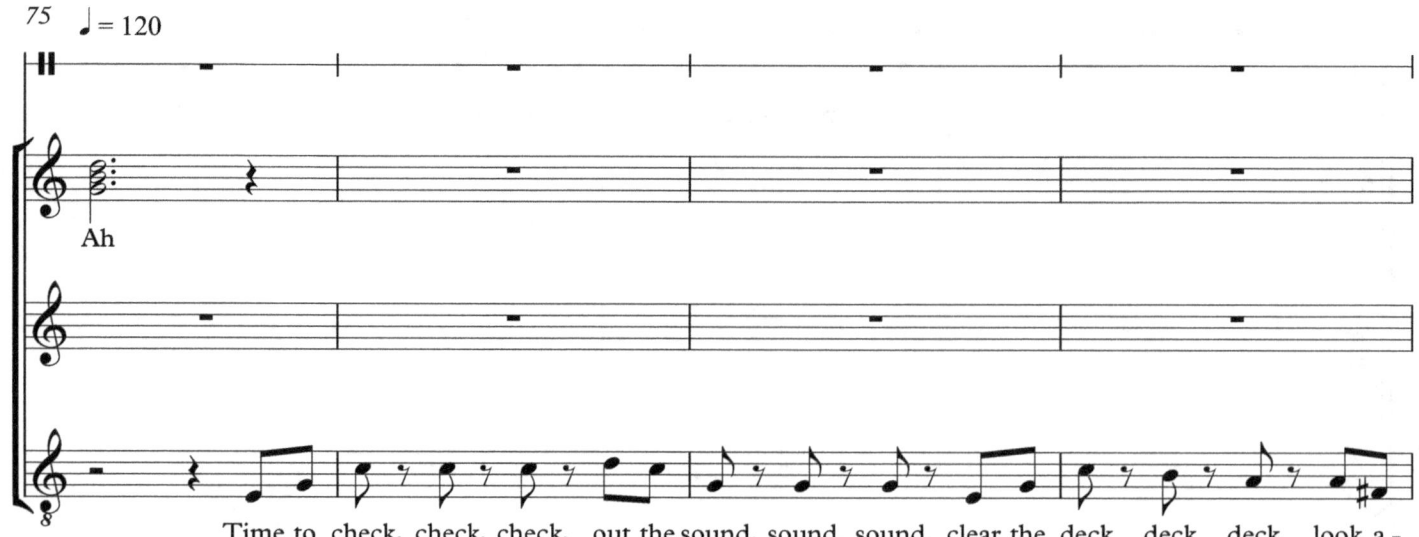
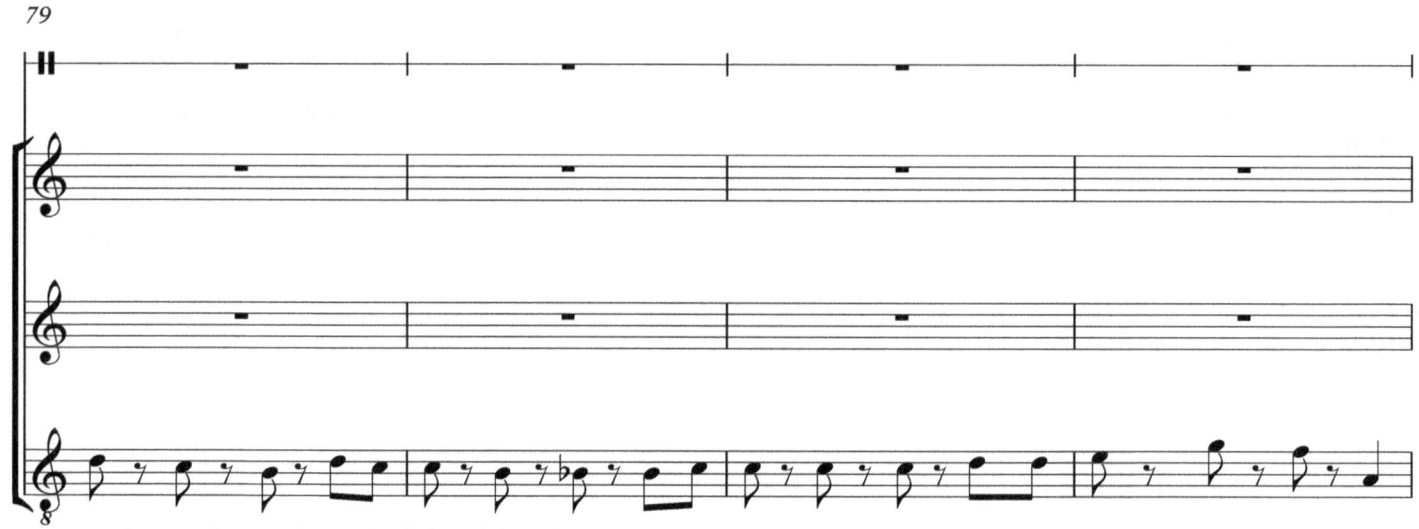

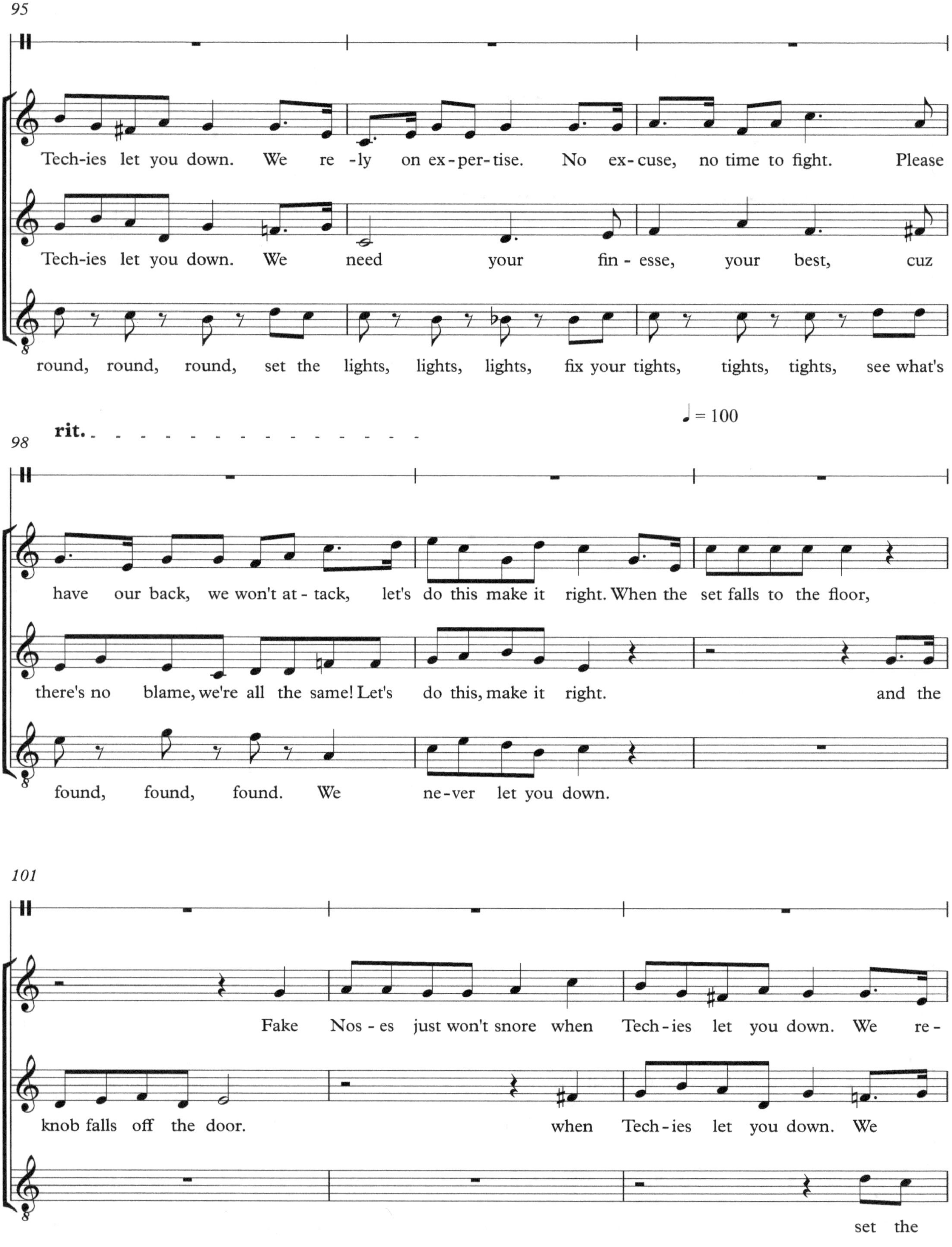
95
Tech-ies let you down. We re -ly on ex-per-tise. No ex-cuse, no time to fight. Please
Tech-ies let you down. We need your fin - esse, your best, cuz
round, round, round, set the lights, lights, lights, fix your tights, tights, tights, see what's
98
rit.
♩ = 100
have our back, we won't at - tack, let's do this make it right. When the set falls to the floor,
there's no blame, we're all the same! Let's do this, make it right. and the
found, found, found. We ne-ver let you down.
101
Fake Nos - es just won't snore when Tech - ies let you down. We re -
knob falls off the door. when Tech - ies let you down. We
set the

14. Starz-Finale

Amy Shojai/Frank Steele

Amy Shojai/Frank Steele

This ma-gic that we weave,

It's not just make be-lieve.

We're art-ists young and old, that's how our stor-y's told, and you com-plete the tale.

We're art-ists young and old, that's how our stor-y's told, and you com-plete the tale.

When au-di-ence be-lieves

We're giv-en a re-prieve.

For-give the al-le-

For-give the al-le-

Copyright © 2017

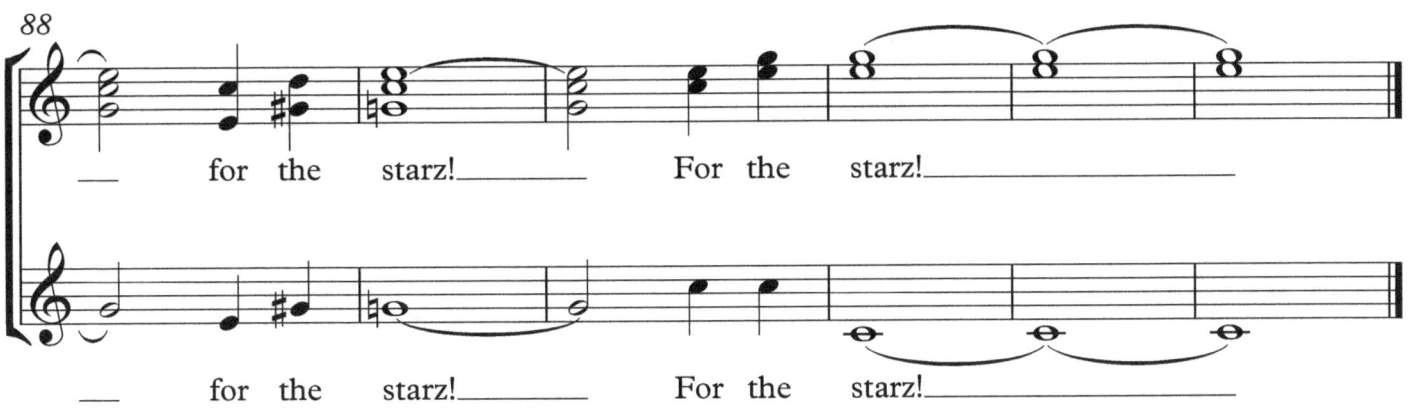

www.ingramcontent.com/pod-product-compliance
Lightning Source LLC
Chambersburg PA
CBHW081350080526
44588CB00016B/2436